PET LAW

by
Margaret C. Jasper

Oceana's Legal Almanac Series:
Law for the Layperson

Oceana Publications

Information contained in this work has been obtained by Oceana Publications from sources believed to be reliable. However, neither the Publisher nor its authors guarantee the accuracy or completeness of any information published herein, and neither the Publisher nor its authors shall be responsible for any errors, omissions or damages arising from the use of this information. This work is published with the understanding that the Publisher and its authors are supplying information, but are not attempting to render legal or other professional services. If such services are required, the assistance of an appropriate professional should be sought.

You may order this or any other Oxford University Press publication by visiting the Oxford University Press and Oceana websites at www.oup.com and www.oceanalaw.com respectively.

Library of Congress Control Number: 2006935505

ISBN 0-19-532365-3
ISBN 978-0-19-532365-8

Oceana's Legal Almanac Series: Law for the Layperson
ISSN 1075-7376

©2007 Oxford University Press, Inc.

Manufactured in the United States of America on acid-free paper.

To My Husband Chris

Your love and support
are my motivation and inspiration

-and-

In memory of my son, Jimmy

Table of Contents

CHAPTER 6:
PET HEALTH ISSUES

ABOUT THE AUTHOR

MARGARET C. JASPER is an attorney engaged in the general practice of law in South Salem, New York, concentrating in the areas of personal injury and entertainment law. Ms. Jasper holds a Juris Doctor degree from Pace University School of Law, White Plains, New York, is a member of the New York and Connecticut bars, and is certified to practice before the United States District Courts for the Southern and Eastern Districts of New York, the United States Court of Appeals for the Second Circuit, and the United States Supreme Court.

Ms. Jasper has been appointed to the law guardian panel for the Family Court of the State of New York, is a member of a number of professional organizations and associations, and is a New York State licensed real estate broker operating as Jasper Real Estate, in South Salem, New York.

Margaret Jasper maintains a website at http://www.JasperLawOffice.com.

In 2004, Ms. Jasper successfully argued a case before the New York Court of Appeals, which gives mothers of babies who are stillborn due to medical negligence the right to bring a legal action and recover emotional distress damages. This successful appeal overturned a 26-year old New York case precedent, which previously prevented mothers of stillborn babies from suing their negligent medical providers.

Ms. Jasper is the author and general editor of the following legal almanacs:

AIDS Law
The Americans with Disabilities Act
Animal Rights Law
Auto Leasing
Bankruptcy Law for the Individual Debtor
Banks and their Customers
Becoming a Citizen

Buying and Selling Your Home
Commercial Law
Consumer Rights Law
Co-ops and Condominiums: Your Rights and Obligations As Owner
Copyright Law
Credit Cards and the Law
Custodial Rights
Dealing with Debt
Dictionary of Selected Legal Terms
Drunk Driving Law
DWI, DUI and the Law
Education Law
Elder Law
Employee Rights in the Workplace
Employment Discrimination Under Title VII
Environmental Law
Estate Planning
Everyday Legal Forms
Executors and Personal Representatives: Rights and
    Responsibilities
Harassment in the Workplace
Health Care and Your Rights
Hiring Household Help and Contractors: Your Rights and Obliga-
    tions Under the Law
Home Mortgage Law Primer
Hospital Liability Law
How To Change Your Name
How To Protect Your Challenged Child
How To Start Your Own Business
Identity Theft and How To Protect Yourself
Individual Bankruptcy and Restructuring
Injured on the Job: Employee Rights, Worker's Compensation and
    Disability Insurance Law
International Adoption
Juvenile Justice and Children's Law
Labor Law
Landlord-Tenant Law
Law for the Small Business Owner
The Law of Attachment and Garnishment
The Law of Buying and Selling
The Law of Capital Punishment
The Law of Child Custody
The Law of Contracts
The Law of Debt Collection

The Law of Dispute Resolution
The Law of Immigration
The Law of Libel and Slander
The Law of Medical Malpractice
The Law of No-Fault Insurance
The Law of Obscenity and Pornography
The Law of Personal Injury
The Law of Premises Liability
The Law of Product Liability
The Law of Speech and the First Amendment
The Law of Violence Against Women
Lemon Laws
Living Together: Practical Legal Issues
Living Wills
Marriage and Divorce
Missing and Exploited Children: How to Protect Your Child
Motor Vehicle Law
Nursing Home Negligence
Patent Law
Pet Law
Prescription Drugs
Privacy and the Internet: Your Rights and Expectations Under the Law
Probate Law
Real Estate Law for the Homeowner and Broker
Religion and the Law
Retirement Planning
The Right to Die
Rights of Single Parents
Small Claims Court
Social Security Law
Special Education Law
Teenagers and Substance Abuse
Trademark Law
Trouble Next Door: What to do With Your Neighbor
Victim's Rights Law
Welfare: Your Rights and the Law
What if It Happened to You: Violent Crimes and Victims' Rights
What if the Product Doesn't Work: Warranties & Guarantees
Workers' Compensation Law
Your Child's Legal Rights: An Overview
Your Rights in a Class Action Suit
Your Rights as a Tenant
Your Rights Under the Family and Medical Leave Act
You've Been Fired: Your Rights and Remedies

INTRODUCTION

Americans have a very special relationship with their pets. The most common types of animals kept as pets are dogs, cats, birds, and fish. Many pets serve dual purposes. For example, dogs act as both companions and workers—e.g., guard dogs, seeing-eye dogs, and hunters—and cats are useful in getting rid of rodents. In more rural areas, animals raised as "pet stock" include chickens, pigs, pigeons and rabbits and are considered both pets and a food source for the family.

Government regulations restrict the types of animals one may keep as a pet. For example, it is illegal to keep certain types of exotic or wild animals as pets. There are a number of good reasons for these restrictions: Wild animals carry diseases that may be transmitted to domestic pets and humans. In addition, such animals often become aggressive due to their inability to cope with an unfamiliar environment.

Owning a pet is a very serious undertaking. Pets depend on their owners for their very survival. Depending on the type of animal, the owner's responsibility may extend for months or years. For example, cats and dogs—the most common household pets—usually live for 15 to 20 years or more, whereas hamsters, gerbils and fish have a much shorter lifespan. It is not an inexpensive task to properly care for a pet. The average cost of basic food, supplies, medical care and training for a dog or cat is $400 to $700 annually.

Pet owners are legally required to take proper care of their animals, making sure they have adequate food and shelter. In addition, as set forth in this almanac, pet owners must make sure they follow all of the laws and regulations governing pet ownership. For example, dogs must be registered and licensed with the proper authority, and must be given all of the required vaccinations. In addition, your pet must not pose a danger or nuisance to others.

This almanac presents an overview of the law as it relates to pet ownership, including the right to own and house certain pets; the prohibition on cruelty; the laws governing travel with pets; animal importation; disease transmission prevention; impounded pets; pet custody; estate planning for your pet; licensing and leash laws; nuisance laws; and the owner's liability for harboring a dangerous animal.

The Appendix provides applicable statutes, sample forms, and other pertinent information and data. The Glossary contains definitions of many of the terms used throughout the almanac.

CHAPTER 1:
PET OWNERSHIP

OWNERSHIP STATISTICS

Approximately 60 percent of all American families have at least one pet in their household. The most common types of animals kept as pets are dogs, cats, birds, and fish. Dogs and cats are the most COMMON pets in America. According to the Humane Society of the United States, there are about 65 million dogs and 77.6 million cats kept as household pets in the United States. Thirty-nine percent of American households—40.6 million—own at least one dog. Most of those households—65%—own one dog, 23% own two dogs, and 12% own three or more dogs. Slightly more male dogs are owned than female dogs. Thirty-four percent of American households—35.4 million—own at least one cat. Half of those households—51%—own one cat, and the rest own two or more cats. Slightly more female cats are owned than male cats.

ACQUIRING YOUR PET

The majority of pets are obtained from friends, acquaintances, and family members. Less than 10% of dogs and cats are purchased from pet shops, 10-20% are purchased from breeders. Eighteen percent of dogs and 16% of cats were adopted from an animal shelter. At least 20% of cats are acquired as strays, many of which were lost and unable to be returned due to lack of identification.

PET ADOPTION

There are many pets available for adoption at shelters and rescue missions. Open access shelters take in all strays and are usually county or city shelters. Humane societies operate private facilities, some of which have open access and some that are more limited. Generally, you can expect to pay an adoption fee that varies according to the services provided.

Animal Shelters

There are between 4,000 and 6,000 animal shelters in the United States. These shelters always have pets available for adoption. Every year, approximately six to eight million dogs and cats enter animal shelters. Of course, there is a greater selection of more mature animals, but you can also find kittens and puppies. In addition, purebred animals make up 25% to 30% of the dogs available at shelters for adoption. Approximately three to four million cats and dogs are adopted from shelters each year; nevertheless, one-half of all animals in animal shelters eventually have to be euthanized because there are not enough people willing to adopt a pet.

Shelter animals are routinely screened for health issues and temperament problems. They are usually vaccinated, spayed and neutered after entering the shelter. Shelter employees attempt to match the animals with potential owners. Owners are generally provided adoption counselling, and offered assistance concerning training and medical services.

Under most state laws, if the animal shelter has not yet sterilized the animal being adopted, the shelter will require the new owner to have the pet spayed or neutered. If the animal is being released for adoption prior to sterilization, the owner must sign an agreement stating that they will have the animal sterilized. In addition, the owner may have to leave a monetary deposit with the shelter which can only be returned once proof of sterilization has been provided. A minority of jurisdictions require mandatory spaying or neutering of all pets unless the owner acquires a special permit.

Purebred Rescue Groups

If you are looking to adopt a purebred, there are rescue groups that offer purebred animals. They are usually operated by people who have knowledge of the breed they offer for adoption. The purebred animals come from failed breeding operations, or were abandoned at boarding kennels and veterinary clinics. Some of the animals were rescued as strays.

BUYING FROM A BREEDER

If you want to purchase a purebred dog and cannot find the right dog through a shelter or rescue group, you should purchase your pet from a reputable breeder. As more fully discussed below, pet shops often obtain their dog population from puppy mills, which are overpopulated and frequent violators of animal anti-cruelty statutes, therefore, purchasing a pet from a pet shop is not recommended.

Many individuals offer dogs for sale to the public directly from their home. They are often amateur breeders looking to make some money. Many of these dogs are offered on the Internet or advertised in newspapers, and there is no way potential buyers can witness the often horrific conditions in which the animals are kept. Therefore, it is crucial that you obtain a referral for a reputable breeder from a reliable source, such as your veterinarian or the American Kennel Club (AKC).

According to The Humane Society of the United States, a good breeder should meet the following minimum requirements:

1. The breeder keeps the dogs in the home as part of the family—-not outside in kennel runs.

2. The breeder has dogs who appear happy and healthy, are excited to meet new people and don't shy away from visitors

3. The breeder shows you where the dogs spend most of their time—in a clean, well-maintained area.

4. The breeder encourages you to spend time with the puppy's parents—-at a minimum, the pup's mother—-when you visit.

5. The breeder only breeds one or two types of dogs and is knowledgeable about what are called "breed standards" –i.e., the desired characteristics of the breed, such as size, proportion, coat, color, and temperament.

6. The breeder has a strong relationship with a local veterinarian and shows you records of veterinary visits for the puppies and explains the puppies' medical history and what vaccinations your new puppy will need.

7. The breeder explains in detail the potential genetic problems inherent in the breed and provides documentation—-through organizations such as the Orthopedic Foundation for Animals—that the puppy's parents and grandparents have been tested to ensure that they are free of genetic problems.

8. The breeder offers guidance for caring for and training your puppy and is available for assistance after you take your puppy home.

9. The breeder provides references from other families who have purchased puppies.

10. The breeder feeds high quality "premium" brand pet food to the puppies.

11. The breeder doesn't always have puppies available but rather will keep a list of interested people for the next available litter.

12. The breeder is actively involved with local, state, and national clubs that specialize in the specific breed, and may compete the dogs in (i) conformation trials, which judge how closely dogs match their breed standard; (ii) obedience trials, which judge how well dogs perform specific sets of tasks on command; and/or tracking and agility trials.

13. The breeder encourages multiple visits and wants your entire family to meet the puppy.

14. The breeder provides you with a written contract and health guarantee and allows plenty of time for you to read it thoroughly.

15. The breeder should not require that you use a specific veterinarian.

The reader is advised that purebred registration papers only provide the recorded lineage of a dog. Although the accuracy of the reported lineage cannot be guaranteed, you can obtain additional information from The American Kennel Club (AKC), which operates the most widely recognized purebred dog registry.

BUYING FROM A PET SHOP

Many individuals purchase their animals from local pet shops. According to the Pet Industry Joint Advisory Council (PIJAC), approximately 3,500 to 3,700 of the 11,500 to 12,000 American pet shops sell cats and dogs. The PIJAC also estimates that pet stores sell 300,000 to 400,000 puppies every year.

Purebreds are available from pet shops; however, they are often bought from puppy and kitten mills, which raise health and safety concerns. These mills are notorious for overbreeding and overcrowding, inbreeding, poor health care, poor food quality, lack of adequate shelter, and lack of socialization. The animals are not properly tested or cared for and, as a result, many of the animals harbor serious genetic problems and other medical problems. Thus, new owners are left to deal with large veterinary bills to treat their pet's health problems.

Although these breeding mills violate animal anti-cruelty laws and the federal *Animal Welfare Act* (AWA), there are not enough resources to properly inspect all of the puppy mills. Therefore, purchasers of dogs from pet shops do so at their own peril.

As of 2001, 17 states had enacted "lemon laws" that permit consumers to receive a refund for the purchase price of a sick puppy. In addition, the consumer is entitled to reimbursement of any veterinary bills incurred due to the puppy's medical condition. If your puppy appears to be suffering from a medical condition, you can file a breeder complaint form with The Humane Society of the United States, and send copies of the complaint to the Department of Agriculture for the state in which the breeder does business; the Attorney General of the state in which the breeder resides and in your state; and to the Better Business Bureau.

A Breeder Complaint Form is set forth at Appendix 1 of this almanac.

THE OVERPOPULATION PROBLEM

Due to uncontrolled breeding of pets, thousands of puppies and kittens are born each day that do not have adequate food, shelter and health care. The number of potential births are staggering. According to the Humane Society of the United States, a fertile dog can produce an average of two litters in one year. The average number of puppies in a litter ranges from six to ten. Thus, in six years, one female dog and her offspring can theoretically produce 67,000 dogs.

For cats, the numbers are even more overwhelming. For example, a fertile cat can produce an average of three litters in one year. The average number of kittens in a litter ranges from four to six. Thus, in seven years, one female cat and her offspring can theoretically produce 420,000 cats. In addition to dogs and cats, rabbits reproduce faster than dogs or cats and rank third in the number of animals who end up in animal shelters.

Between six and eight million unwanted dogs and cats enter animal shelters each year, and three to four million of these animals must be euthanized because there are not enough households to adopt them all. Stray animals that are left on the street pose public health and safety problems, and the cost of capturing, housing, and feeding this overabundance of unwanted animals becomes a burden on taxpayers.

SPAYING AND NEUTERING PROGRAMS

Animal welfare organizations have called for the implementation of a widespread spaying and neutering program to try and reduce the overpopulation problem. Female dogs and cats are spayed by removing their reproductive organs. Male dogs and cats are neutered by removing their testicles. The procedures are performed humanely while the animal is under sedation.

Spaying and neutering animals not only assists in solving the overpopulation problem, thus reducing costs, it also provides health benefits to the animals. Experts agree that dogs and cats that have been spayed and neutered live longer and have fewer health problems. In addition, pets that have been spayed and neutered are generally more affectionate, have better temperaments and are less likely to bite. In those jurisdictions that have started such programs, the number of dogs and cats entering animal shelters has decreased and a lot less innocent animals are euthanized as a result.

If you are interested in having your pet spayed or neutered, you should contact your veterinarian. If the cost is an issue, you can contact your local animal shelter and find out whether there are any clinics that offer these services at a reduced price. Spay/USA is a national referral network that may be able to provide a referral and additional information and can be reached by calling 1-800-248-SPAY or online at www.spayusa.org.

PET CUSTODY DISPUTES

It may sound impractical, but fighting over the custody of an animal can be an expensive and time-consuming undertaking when joint owners of a beloved pet decide to separate or divorce. Historically, pets were treated like personal property and subject to equitable distribution of property rules in a divorce proceeding. However, a trend is emerging where some pet owners, who consider their pets as family members rather than mere property, are seeking rights similar to those sought by parents over their children, including "custody, visitation and support" rights. They argue that there is an emotional bond with the pet that goes beyond any attachment to mere personal property. Case law on this issue is unsettled, with some states awarding custody and visitation of family pets, and other states refusing to upgrade the status of a pet from that of personal property to a higher standing.

CHAPTER 2:
"NO-PET" LEASE CLAUSES

IN GENERAL

When you own your own home, nobody can tell you whether or not you can own a pet. But when you rent, it's a whole different story. For a variety of reasons, many landlords simply do not want tenants to have pets living in their rental property, and you generally must abide by any no-pet clause contained in your lease. Most landlords overlook small pets, such as fish, birds, hamsters, etc., and some will even make an exception for cats and small dogs.

No-pet clauses are usually enforced against dogs and, unfortunately, this is one of the biggest reasons many pet owners give for surrendering their canine companions to animal shelters. Irresponsible pet ownership—e.g., owners who let their dogs damage property, bark incessantly at all hours, and intimidate tenants—is a big reason that landlords have instituted no-pet clauses in their lease. Landlords do not want to have to repair damage, listen to complaints from other tenants, or risk liability if a tenant's dog bites someone on the landlord's property.

LANDLORD LIABILITY

In general, a landlord would not be liable to a third party for injuries caused by a tenant's dog unless one of the following scenarios exist:

ACTUAL KNOWLEDGE

In most cases, a landlord will not be held liable unless the landlord knew that the tenant's dog was a threat to the safety of others, and failed to take the necessary steps within his or her power to have the dog removed from the premises. The law requires that the landlord have actual knowledge of the dog's dangerous propensities unless the particular breed of dog—e.g., a pit bull or rotweiller—falls under a category that creates a presumption of risk pursuant to local regulations.

Actual knowledge may be demonstrated if, for example, the landlord knew that the dog had bitten someone in the past. Nevertheless, some states do not hold the landlord liable even if he or she knew that the tenant's dog was potentially harmful. Of course, to be held responsible, it must be shown that the landlord had the power and authority to have the dog removed, e.g. the landlord had the right to exercise a no-pet clause in the tenant's lease and failed to do so.

CONTROL OVER TENANT'S DOG

A landlord will not be held liable for injuries caused by a tenant's dog unless it can be shown that the landlord exercised some custody or control over the tenant's dog. For example, if the landlord allowed the dog to roam free on the property, or used the dog for security purposes on the premises, etc., a court may assess some degree of responsibility against the landlord.

NEGOTIATING A NO-PET CLAUSE

Even if your lease contains a pet restriction, you may be able to negotiate the no-pet clause with your landlord if you can demonstrate that your dog is well-behaved, and you are a responsible pet owner. You will likely, however, have to agree to certain additional provisions in your lease that address the landlord's valid concerns, and provide proof that your dog won't misbehave. For example, your landlord may require you to repair any damage caused by your dog, or to pay an additional deposit or higher rent in order to offset any damages your pet may cause.

Your landlord may also allow you to keep the dog you presently own, but refuse to allow you to bring in any replacement pets in the future. In addition, the landlord may require you to carry some type of liability insurance in case your dog bites someone, and indemnify the landlord for any damages awarded in a personal injury lawsuit.

If your pet lived with you at your previous residences, it would strengthen your case if you provide your new landlord with letters from your previous landlords and/or neighbors attesting to the fact that your pet never caused any problems. You should also provide proof that your dog is properly licensed and vaccinated. If your dog has had any special training, such as obedience school, provide the landlord with copies of his or her certificate. Offer to bring your dog with you so the landlord can observe the animal's behavior. You can take this opportunity to demonstrate your dog's ability to follow your commands. This is when obedience training comes in handy.

If you are successful in convincing your landlord that your dog will not cause any problems, and your landlord agrees to allow you to keep your pet, make sure you get a waiver of the no-pet clause put in your lease in case the landlord tries to change his or her mind after you have moved into your new home, or sells the rental property to another owner who may want to strictly enforce the no-pet clause.

GOING TO COURT

If all efforts at negotiation have failed, and you are adamant about living in rental property that contains a no-pet clause in your lease, you may be able to obtain a court order allowing you to keep your pet if you can demonstrate that circumstances exist making the restriction unenforceable. Nevertheless, a tenant is not advised to acquire a pet if he or she knows this is a violation of the lease.

SECURITY CONCERNS

If you can prove you need your pet for security reasons, you may be able to argue that you are entitled to a waiver of the no-pet clause. This argument may prevail if the property is in a high crime area, the landlord has not taken the proper safety precautions to secure the building, and you contend that you need the dog for protection.

ESTOPPEL

A landlord cannot add a no-pet clause to your lease after you have already signed your lease. In addition, if the landlord told you that you could keep your dog, you may be able to challenge an eviction based on the owner's acquiescence. Further, if your pet has been living with you openly and with the knowledge of the landlord for a certain period of time and the landlord did not try to enforce the no-pet clause of the lease, a court may allow you to keep your pet.

Under the estoppel doctrine, the landlord may not be permitted to exercise a no-pet clause at a later date on the basis that he implicitly approved by failing to take steps to enforce the clause, thus waiving his claim by his inaction.

SPECIAL PROVISIONS FOR THE ELDERLY AND DISABLED

Another scenario in which a no-pet clause may be unenforceable concerns trained assistance dogs, such as seeing eye dogs owned by disabled tenants and companion animals owned by senior citizens.

Numerous studies have shown that pets can be extremely beneficial to the health of the aging population, leading to lower blood pressure, increased motor skills, and mental stimulation.

APPLICABLE LAW

Whether or not a tenant will be permitted to keep a pet despite the landlord's "no pet" policy depends in large part on the law which governs the specific problem. A tenant's rights may be regulated by federal, state or local laws. Federal law applies to everyone in the United States and the violation of a federal law is illegal in every state. Federal law determines the minimum protection available to a tenant in rental housing and generally concerns a tenant's civil rights in housing, such as a prohibition against discriminatory practices. State law can provide further specific protections for tenants under the state constitution and statutes enacted by the state legislature however state law cannot provide a tenant with less protection than the federal law requires. Municipal and local laws provide even more specific regulations.

Federal Law

In recognition of the medical benefits discussed above, elderly and disabled tenants in federally-subsidized housing are allowed to own pets, and landlords must make reasonable accommodations for their disabled tenants. A reasonable accommodation may include allowing a disabled tenant to keep a pet provided it does not cause an undue hardship on the landlord. There are four federal laws that may impact an elderly or disabled tenant's right to keep a companion animal in rental housing.

The Housing and Urban Rural Recovery Act of 1983

Under *The Housing and Urban Rural Recovery Act*, the owner or manager of any federally assisted rental housing that is designated for the elderly or disabled cannot prohibit a tenant from keeping a common household pet.

The Act provides that:

> No owner or manager of any federally assisted rental housing for the elderly or handicapped may—
>
> > (1) as a condition of tenancy or otherwise, prohibit or prevent any tenant in such housing from owning common household pets or having common household pets living in the dwelling accommodations of such tenant in such housing; or

(2) restrict or discriminate against any such person in connection with admission to, or continued occupancy of, such housing by reason of the ownership of such pets by, or the presence of such pets in the dwelling accommodations of, such person.

Nevertheless, the statute does permit a landlord to remove an animal who is considered a threat or nuisance to others, thus the owner of a companion animal in such rental housing should make a special effort to ensure that their pet behaves appropriately and receives proper care.

In that connection, the Act provides that:

Nothing in this section may be construed to prohibit any owner or manager of federally assisted rental housing for the elderly or handicapped, or any local housing authority or other appropriate authority of the community where such housing is located, from requiring the removal of any such housing of any pet whose conduct or condition is duly determined to constitute a nuisance or a threat to the health or safety of the other occupants of such housing or of other persons in the community where such housing is located.

The Fair Housing Amendments Act of 1988

Under *The Fair Housing Amendments Act,* it is illegal to refuse to sell or rent a dwelling to a person because of race, color, religion, sex, familial status, or national origin. These prohibitions against discrimination form the basis for permitting persons with disabilities to keep a companion animal in their home when the animal is needed to provide assistance to the disabled tenant. For example, a landlord cannot refuse to rent to, or evict, a blind person because they own a seeing eye dog. Further, the law applies whether or not the disabled individual is the person named on the lease provided the disabled individual is legally living in the dwelling.

The Fair Housing Amendments Act applies to nearly all housing, whether the dwelling is for sale or rent, but generally excludes (i) buildings with four or fewer units if the landlord lives in the building; and (ii) private owners who own fewer than three single family homes.

The Americans With Disabilities Act of 1990

The Americans With Disabilities Act (ADA) also requires public agencies, or agencies receiving federal funds, to provide access for all individuals, regardless of disability. Disabled individuals who need their companion animal as part of their care, treatment or rehabilitation may also rely on this statute as a basis for keeping their pet in their rental home.

The Rehabilitation Act of 1973

The Rehabilitation Act—the predecessor to the ADA—provides similar protection to disabled persons when the landlord is connected with a federally funded program.

State and Local Laws

Some state and local laws provide the same protection to elderly and disabled tenants living in private housing concerning the right to keep companion animals. However, as set forth above, state and local laws can provide its citizens greater rights than those provided under federal law, but their protections cannot fall below the minimum federal standards. For example, a state may pass laws that give greater protection to the elderly or disabled, much like the federal legislation described above, but cannot place limitations on the protections afforded under the federal law.

THE UNITED STATES DEPARTMENT OF HOUSING AND URBAN DEVELOPMENT (HUD)

The United States Department of Housing and Urban Development enforces the federal fair housing laws and provides information and assistance in making a complaint. The National HUD Discrimination Hotline is 1-800-669-9777/TDD: 1-800 927-9275. In addition, the Fair Housing Information Clearinghouse provides educational materials about fair housing regulations and can be reached at 1-800-343-3442/TDD: 1-800-290-1617.

CHAPTER 3:
PET LICENSING AND LEASH LAWS

LICENSING REQUIREMENTS

Most laws require both cats and dogs to be licensed, and that your pets wear their license tags at all times. Licensing is an important element in animal control and the protection of the public health. Information about licensed dogs assists in the medical follow-up of persons potentially exposed to infected dogs. Licensing also helps to reunite lost dogs with their owners.

A license is generally obtained from your state, county or local animal licensing authority—e.g., your county or town clerk—after you have demonstrated that your pet has been properly vaccinated against rabies. If you do not obtain a license for your pet as required by law, you may be fined.

A typical animal licensing law under the New York City Health Code is as follows:

Title 24 § 161.04 Dog Licenses

(b) Every person who owns, possesses or controls a dog shall not permit it to be in any public place, or in any open or unfenced area abutting on a public place, unless the dog has a collar about its neck with a currently valid metal tag attached thereto bearing the number of the license obtained for such dog. (24 RCNY Health Code Reg. § 161.04)

In order to obtain a license, you must generally provide proof that your pet has been vaccinated against rabies. Puppies and kittens do not have to be vaccinated until they reach the age of about 3 months. Your veterinarian will provide you with a completed and signed rabies certificate for your records, a copy of which is provided to the licensing authority. The rabies certificate shows when and where your pet was vaccinated, and provides important ownership information in case the animal becomes lost or stolen.

Pet licenses are usually valid for one year from the date of the pet's rabies vaccination. For example, if you have your pet vaccinated against rabies and purchase the license on June 1st, the license is valid for one full year until June 1st of the following year. However, if you have your pet vaccinated on May 1st but you don't purchase the license until June 1st, the license will only be valid for 11 months, until May 1st of the following year, instead of a full year.

The cost of a pet license ranges from approximately $10 to $25, depending on whether your pet has been sterilized. If the animal has not been spayed or neutered, the cost is generally higher. Some states have substantially higher rates for pets that are not spayed or neutered as a way of encouraging pet owners to sterilize their animals and help prevent overpopulation and overcrowding of animal shelters. A minority of jurisdictions require mandatory spaying or neutering of all pets unless the owner acquires a special permit. The licensing charge for assistance dogs, such as seeing eye dogs, is generally waived. If your pet's license is lost, you must purchase a replacement license at a nominal charge.

It is important to make sure your pet wears their license at all times, particularly if your pet spends time outside the home, so that your pet can be properly identified if it is lost or stolen. A licensed pet is more likely to be returned to its owner if it is lost. Unlicensed pets often end up in shelters, where they may be euthanized if not claimed or adopted within a certain period of time.

In addition, the license demonstrates to the public that your pet has been vaccinated against rabies. The rabies vaccine protects your pet from contracting this deadly disease, and protects you, your family, and anyone else who comes in contact with your dog. Without proof of vaccination, if your dog becomes lost and bites someone, there is no way for the bite victim to know whether your dog has been vaccinated, therefore, the victim will have to undergo rabies treatment unnecessarily.

The rabies disease is discussed more fully in Chapter 6 of this almanac.

Most pet owners recognize the importance of licensing their dogs, but question the necessity of licensing an "indoor" cat. However, licensing authorities agree that a license for your indoor cat is even more important than for an "outdoor" cat that frequently travels outside the home and knows the area. An "indoor" cat that somehow escapes is more likely to get lost because it is not familiar with the neighborhood.

LEASH LAWS

Most jurisdictions require that dog owners have their dog on a leash when walking the dog in public or in an open area. It is a violation for any person to permit their dog to be "at large." A typical animal leash law under the New York City Health Code is as follows:

Title 24 § 161.05 Dog to be restrained

A person who owns, possesses or controls a dog shall not permit it to be in any public place or in any open or unfenced area abutting on a public place unless the dog is effectively restrained by a leash or chain not more than six feet long. (24 RCNY Health Code Reg. § 161.05)

At Large

The term "at large" refers to an animal that is not under the physical control of a person by means of a leash, cord or chain, or not in the physical presence of its owner or other person responsible for the animal. "At large" also refers to a dog that is not confined to the property of its owner by means of a fence. It is also against the law to tie, chain or tether a dog to public property or property belonging to another person.

If a dog is found "at large" by an animal control officer, and the dog does not have a license or other means of identification, it is generally transported to an animal shelter. If the dog is licensed, the animal control officer may return the dog to its residence and issue a citation to the pet's owner.

In general, cats are considered free roaming animals, and are not required to be confined on a leash. However, if a cat poses a nuisance, a property owner may have the right to catch the cat and have it taken to the animal shelter.

Canine Waste Laws

It is generally against the law for any person to allow their pet to defecate on public property and on private property not belonging to the animal's owner unless the dog owner makes every effort to immediately clean up and dispose of their dog's droppings in a sanitary manner. Violators may face penalties for failure to do so. Owners of assistance dogs are usually exempt from these laws.

IMPOUNDMENT

If a dog or cat is impounded while wearing identification, a shelter will generally hold the animal for a certain period of time while trying to notify the owner, or waiting for the owner to claim their pet. If a dog or cat is impounded without identification, the shelter will hold the animal for a shorter period of time while it makes reasonable efforts to notify the owner. Nevertheless, in both cases, the primary responsibility of locating the animal falls upon the pet owner. A number of jurisdictions give their animal control officers the right to destroy a dog that is at large without identification, particularly if it poses a danger to the public, without first attempting to locate the animal's owner.

On occasion, an animal control officer will seize a dog while it is in the owner's possession because the animal is alleged to have bitten someone or is considered a dangerous dog. However, unless there is an emergency that requires the immediate seizure of the dog, the owner must be notified before the dog is seized or destroyed, and must be given an opportunity to challenge the animal control officer's actions in court before the dog is destroyed.

So many dogs enter animal shelters each day that the shelters become overcrowded to the point that they cannot properly feed and house them. Oftentimes, if a dog is not claimed by his or her owner, adopted, or sold within three to five days, the shelter has no choice but to euthanize the dog. Therefore, if you think an animal control officer has picked up your pet, you should contact all of the animal shelters in your area as soon as you become aware that your dog is missing. You should visit all of the shelters in person because oftentimes they are understaffed and you may get misinformation over the telephone.

If you find your dog at a shelter, you will likely have to pay a fine. The shelter will also want to make sure your dog is vaccinated and licensed before your pet will be released to you. So, make sure you bring a copy of your dog's rabies certificate and licensing information with you. In case you are unable to locate your dog at the shelter, you should bring pictures of your dog and/or missing pet fliers containing your contact information to leave in case your dog shows up at the shelter at a later date.

If you find that your dog has been adopted before you had a chance to reclaim it, you may be able to get your dog back if the animal shelter did not try to notify you even though your dog had identification, or if the shelter did not keep your dog for a reasonable period of time after it was picked up. However, if you delay too long, without a good excuse, your dog may be adopted and you may have no right to get your pet back. So, it is of the utmost importance that you act quickly as soon as you become aware that your dog is lost or missing.

If an owner fails to reclaim their dog, and nobody adopts the animal within a short time period, some shelters may be permitted to sell the dog to a research lab for scientific purposes, however, some jurisdictions forbid the sale of animals turned into shelters to be sold to research facilities.

If a dog is not reclaimed by its owner, adopted or sold within a certain time period, the dog is euthanized. The law requires euthanization to be carried out in a quick and humane manner. Although most laws do not specify the manner in which a dog must be destroyed, most shelters use lethal injection as the means to euthanize the animal.

LOST PETS

If your pet is lost, you should check with animal control and the local animal shelters, as more fully discussed above. You should create a flier and leave copies all over the neighborhood as far as you believe your animal could travel, including public bulletin boards. You should also leave copies of the flier with all of the animal shelters in the area, animal rescue organizations, veterinarians, pet shops, and pet grooming services. Ask local businesses if they will allow you to post the flier in their window.

The flier should contain a recent photo of your pet with a detailed description, e.g., size, weight, gender, age, color, breed, etc., including any special markings. Give the date, time, and place your pet went missing, as well as the circumstances surrounding its disappearance. Also include your contact information and any reward you are offering.

CHAPTER 4:
NUISANCE PETS AND DANGEROUS DOG
LAWS

HANDLING A NUISANCE PET PROBLEM

If you live next door to a dog that barks all night, or a cat that regularly rummages through the trash cans on your property, you really can't blame the animals for doing what animals do. You can, however, go to the pet's owner to try and get some relief. It may be that your neighbor is unaware that their pet is causing such a disturbance. If you are on good terms with your neighbor, you can usually work out some type of agreement, e.g., the dog will not be left outside during the overnight hours, or the cat will be restricted to a fenced in area of the yard.

You can also try mediation, if your neighbor is willing to join you, in order to work out some mutually satisfactory solution with the assistance of an impartial mediator. Mediators are trained to help individuals focus on the disputed issues and make constructive suggestions on how to solve the problem without letting the discussion escalate into argument.

The topic of mediation is discussed more fully in this author's legal almanac entitled The Law of Dispute Resolution, published by Oceana Publishing Company.

Nevertheless, if you encounter a pet owner who takes a defensive position and is unwilling to fix the problem, there are public nuisance and noise restriction laws in most jurisdictions. You can contact animal control authorities or the local police and ask them to enforce these laws. A typical animal nuisance law under the New York City Health Code is as follows:

TITLE 24 § 161.03 CONTROL OF DOGS AND OTHER ANIMALS TO PREVENT NUISANCE

(a) A person who owns, possesses or controls a dog, cat or other animal shall not permit the animal to commit a nuisance on a sidewalk of any public place, on a floor, wall, stairway or roof of any public or private premises used in common by the public, or on a fence, wall or stairway of a building abutting on a public place. (24 RCNY Health Code Reg. § 161.03)

If all else fails, you may have to bring a nuisance lawsuit in small claims court, however, suing your neighbor can be time consuming, costly and an unpleasant experience, and should only be used as your last resort. If you prove your case in court, the judge may fine the pet owner, and/or may issue an order setting forth certain conditions concerning the offending dog, e.g. mandatory obedience training. If the animal destroyed property belonging to you, you may be able to recover monetary damages.

More detailed information on bringing a small claims case may be found in this author's legal almanac entitled *Small Claims Court,* published by Oceana Publishing Company.

DOG BITE LIABILITY

Every year, more than 4.7 million people are bitten by dogs, may of whom require medical intervention for their injuries. If a dog bites, the owner is usually held liable if: (i) the owner knew the dog had a tendency to bite; (ii) there is a state statute that makes the owner liable regardless of whether or not the owner knew the dog had a tendency to bite (a "strict liability" statute); or (iii) the owner was unreasonably careless. The owner is liable not only for dog bites, but for any other injuries that the dog may cause.

A number of jurisdictions have what is known as the "one bite rule." Basically, this rule means that a dog owner is only liable for injuries caused by their dog if he or she knew that the dog was likely to bite someone. Once a dog bites someone, or tries to bite someone, the owner is automatically placed on notice that the dog is a biter, and the owner will be liable for any future injuries caused by the dog.

The following jurisdictions follow the "one bite" rule: Alaska, Arkansas, Colorado, Delaware, Georgia, Idaho, Kansas, Maryland, Mississippi, Missouri, Nevada, New Mexico, New York, North Carolina, North Dakota, Oregon, South Dakota, Tennessee, Texas, Vermont, Virginia, and Wyoming.

The dog's owner will generally be responsible for the costs the victim incurs as a result of being bitten, such as medical bills, lost wages, and the victim's pain and suffering. Homeowner's insurance usually covers a dog bite claim, however, as more fully discussed below, many insurance companies are refusing to insure homeowners who harbor certain breeds of dogs that are considered inherently dangerous.

As more fully discussed below, if a complaint is brought against the dog to determine whether it should be declared a "dangerous dog," a hearing will determine whether the owner must destroy the dog or whether there will be strict requirements imposed on the owner if he or she wishes to keep the dog.

DEFENSES

Under certain circumstances, a dog owner may not be held liable. For example, liability may be avoided if: (i) the owner can prove that the injured person provoked the injury, e.g., the victim hit or teased the dog, or accidentally hurt the dog; (ii) the victim voluntarily and knowingly risked being injured by the dog, e.g. by ignoring warning signs; (iii) the victim was trespassing or breaking the law; and (iv) the victim was being unreasonably careless around the dog, which contributed to the victim's injury.

Nevertheless, if someone is being attacked by a dog, or witnesses a dog attack, under most state laws, they are permitted to take whatever action is necessary to stop the attack, including killing the dog.

TAKING ACTION FOLLOWING A DOG ATTACK

If you are bitten or otherwise attacked by a dog, make sure you get the name and contact information for the dog's owner and any witnesses of the attack. If the dog does not have a license tag, and you don't know who owned the dog, if at all possible, you should try to capture the dog so it can be tested for rabies. If you cannot capture the dog, make sure you can adequately describe the dog to the animal control officers so they can try and locate the dog.

If you are seriously injured, you should seek immediate medical attention and keep copies of all hospital and medical reports. You should also keep all of the medical bills for which you will be seeking reimbursement from the dog's owner.

The biting incident should be reported to your local animal control office. If the dog did not have license tags, and the owner cannot be located, the dog will likely be confined and quarantined for a period of time to make sure it doesn't have rabies. If the owner is located and able to produce proof that the dog has been vaccinated, confinement is generally not necessary.

You should check with the local animal control office to find out if the dog that bit you ever bit anyone else, or if the dog has been declared a "dangerous dog," as more fully discussed below. If so, this will make your case must stronger if you have to take the dog owner to court to recover damages.

DANGEROUS DOGS

The majority of pet dogs are not dangerous, and if they are involved in a biting incident, it is usually because they were being provoked or they are being protective. Nevertheless, as discussed above, once a dog does bite someone, even if it is a one-time occurrence, there are laws in place in many jurisdictions that intervene to identify whether the dog is a threat to public safety. Some of these laws automatically classify certain dogs as dangerous despite whether they have exhibited aggressive behavior, simply because of their breed, e.g., pit bulls.

This legislative effort in the area of dog regulation is due to increasing reports all across the United States that there are certain exceptionally dangerous and unpredictable dogs of various breeds that, once provoked, become uncontrollable lethal weapons, posing significant dangers to unsuspecting and innocent people. Statistics demonstrate that people die as a result of dog attacks, at the rate of one or more a month, and countless others have been hurt and maimed, with children and elderly persons being the most frequent targets.

In order to protect the health and safety of their citizens, many local jurisdictions have enacted "dangerous dog" laws, intended to identify vicious dogs and prevent injuries. A growing number of states have also enacted dangerous dog laws, including: California, Colorado, Delaware, District of Columbia, Florida, Georgia, Hawaii, Illinois, Kentucky, Louisiana, Maine, Maryland, Massachusetts, Michigan, Minnesota, Nebraska, Nevada, New Hampshire, New Jersey, New York, North Carolina, Ohio, Oklahoma, Pennsylvania, Rhode Island, South Carolina, South Dakota, Texas, Vermont, Virginia, Washington, and West Virginia.

DANGEROUS DOG DESIGNATION

In general, the process of having a dog designated as a dangerous animal begins with a formal complaint about the dog by any person, including an animal control officer or person who has been injured by the dog. A hearing is conducted before a judge or other designated official, and evidence may be presented by all interested persons as to the dog's dangerousness.

Usually, if the dog has already caused severe injury to someone, the dog may be impounded, at the owner's expense, pending the hearing and determination of the complaint. A determination is made, based on the evidence, whether or not the dog falls under the category of a dangerous animal, according to the applicable law.

A typical statutory definition for a "dangerous dog" is set forth in the Administrative Code of New York, as follows:

Title 17 § 17-342 Definitions

c. "Dangerous dog" means any dog that when unprovoked, approaches, or menaces any person in a dangerous or terrorizing manner, or in an apparent attitude of attack, upon the streets, sidewalks, or any public grounds or places; or any dog with a known propensity, tendency or disposition to attack when unprovoked, to cause injury or to otherwise endanger the safety of human beings or domestic animals; or any dog which bites, inflicts injury, assaults or otherwise attacks a human being or domestic animal without provocation on public or private property; or any dog owned or harbored primarily or in part for the purpose of dog fighting or any dog trained for dog fighting.

d. "Severe injury" means any physical injury that results in broken bones or disfiguring lacerations requiring either multiple stitches or cosmetic surgery.

e. "Unprovoked" means that the dog was not hit, kicked, taunted or struck by a person with any object or part of a person's body nor was any part of the dog's body pulled, pinched or squeezed by a person.

(Chapter 3. Administrative Code of the City of New York; Subchapter 6: Dangerous Dog Regulation and Protection)

The law generally excuses dogs if the person who was injured was intentionally trespassing on the dog owner's property, attempting to commit a crime, or was seriously provoking the dog. New York law addresses this exemption, as follows:

Title 17 § 17-347 Excused behavior.

No dog shall be declared dangerous pursuant to 167;17-345 if the threat, injury, or damage caused by such dog was sustained by a person who, at the time, was committing a willful trespass or other tort upon the premises occupied by the owner of the dog, or was tormenting,. abusing, or assaulting the dog, or has, in the past, been observed or reported to have tormented, abused or assaulted the dog, or was committing or attempting to commit a crime. Nor shall any dog be declared dangerous if it was responding to pain or injury, or was protecting itself, its kennels, or its offspring. If the trespass is determined to be of an innocent nature, the commissioner may, depending on the circumstances...find the dog to be dangerous. (Chapter 3. Administrative Code of the City of New York; Subchapter 6: Dangerous Dog Regulation and Protection)

RESTRICTIONS

If a dog receives an official designation as a dangerous dog, there are special restrictions placed on their owners to prevent the dog from causing injuries, ranging from confinement to destruction of the dog, if it cannot be controlled. For example, under the Administrative Code of the City of New York, if, after the hearing, it is determined that the dog is dangerous, the commissioner may order the owner to comply with one or more of the following requirements:

Title 17 § 17-345 Determination of a dangerous dog.

a. Registration. The commissioner may order the owner of a dangerous dog to register such dog with the department. The application for such registration shall contain the name and address of the owner, the breed, age, sex, color, and any other identifying marks of the dog, the location where the dog is to be kept if not at the address of the owner and any other information which the commissioner may require. The application for registration pursuant to this paragraph shall be accompanied by a registration fee of twenty-five dollars. Each dog registered pursuant hereto shall be assigned an official registration number by the department. Such registration number shall be inscribed on a metal tag which shall be attached to the dog's collar at all times. The tag and a certificate of registration shall be of such form and design and shall contain such information as the commissioner shall prescribe and shall be issued to the owner upon payment of the registration fee and the presentment of sufficient evidence that the owner has complied with all of the orders of the commissioner as prescribed at the determination hearing.

b. Muzzling or confinement. The commissioner may order the owner of a dangerous dog to muzzle the dog or confine the dog, at all times, indoors or in a proper enclosure for a dangerous dog which shall consist of a securely enclosed and locked pen or structure, suitable to prevent the entry of young children, or any part of their bodies or other foreign objects, and designed to prevent the animal from escaping. Such pen or structure shall have secure sides and prevent the dog from digging his way out through the bottom. The pen or structure shall also provide the dog with protection from the elements. The owner shall also conspicuously display a sign designed with a warning symbol approved by the commissioner which indicates to both children and adults the presence of a dangerous dog, on the pen or structure and on or near the entrance to the residence where the dog is kept. At any time that the dog is not confined as required herein, the dog shall be muzzled in such a manner as to prevent it from biting or injuring any person, and kept on a leash no longer than six feet with the owner or some other responsible person attending such dog.

c. Liability insurance. The commissioner may order the owner of a dangerous dog to maintain, in full force and effect, a liability insurance policy of one hundred thousand dollars for personal injury or death of any person, resulting from an attack of such dangerous dog.

d. Humane destruction. The commissioner may order the humane destruction of any dog that kills or causes severe injury to a human being, based upon the severity of the injury and the circumstances of the injury.

e. Other remedies. The commissioner may order

(i) that the dog be permanently removed from the city; or

(ii) that the owner and the dog complete a course of obedience and/or anti-bite training approved by the commissioner.

(Chapter 3. Administrative Code of the City of New York; Subchapter 6: Dangerous Dog Regulation and Protection)

VIOLATIONS OF COURT ORDERED-RESTRICTIONS

If the dog's owner violates the court-ordered restrictions, many laws provide that the dog can be seized and impounded, and the owner may be fined and/or imprisoned. For example, the New York law provides as follows:

Title 17 § 17-346 Confiscation and/or confinement of a dangerous dog.

a. In the event that the owner of a dangerous dog violates any order of the commissioner as prescribed at the determination hearing, such owner's dog may be confiscated and impounded by the proper authorities upon the order of the commissioner. In addition, any dog determined to be dangerous shall be immediately confiscated by the proper authorities if the dog bites or attacks a human being and causes injury, or if the dog, at the sufferance of its owner, is engaged in or apparently engaged in a dog fight contest or is approximately near the area in which such a contest is being conducted.

b. The owner of a dog determined to be dangerous by the commissioner, which has been confiscated pursuant to subdivision (a) of this section, may request the commissioner to conduct a hearing to determine if the dog should be returned to the owner. Upon such request, the commissioner shall provide for a hearing within five days.

(Chapter 3. Administrative Code of the City of New York; Subchapter 6: Dangerous Dog Regulation and Protection)

Title 17 § 17-350 Violations and penalties.

a. Any person who violates any provision of this subchapter or any of the regulations promulgated hereunder shall be guilty of a misdemeanor punishable by a fine of not less than five hundred nor more than five thousand dollars or by imprisonment for not more than one year, or both.

b. In addition to the penalties prescribed by subdivision a of this section, any person who violates any of the provisions of this subchapter or any rule or regulation promulgated hereunder shall be liable for a civil penalty of not less than five hundred nor more than five thousand dollars.

(Chapter 3. Administrative Code of the City of New York; Subchapter 6: Dangerous Dog Regulation and Protection)

CREATING A DANGEROUS DOG

If it is found that the pet owner deliberately made a dog vicious for the purpose of fighting or causing injury to others, the owner may face fines and/or imprisonment. The New York law is typical of this prohibition:

Title 17 § 17-343 Acquisition of a dangerous dog prohibited.

a. No person shall own or harbor any dog for the purpose of dog fighting, or train, torment, badger, bait or use any dog for the purpose of causing or encouraging said dog to attack human beings or domestic animals when not provoked. (Chapter 3. Administrative Code of the City of New York; Subchapter 6: Dangerous Dog Regulation and Protection)

If a dog who has been trained to be vicious mauls or kills someone, the owner may be charged with a crime, such as manslaughter or murder.

BREED-SPECIFIC RESTRICTIONS

Dog experts disagree that certain breeds of dogs have inherent vicious tendencies, however, injury reports and lawsuits appear to indicate that certain breeds of dog are responsible for the majority of serious injuries. For this reason, many jurisdictions have passed laws prohibiting the possession of certain breeds, such as pit bulls, that are deemed dangerous. Some jurisdictions do not prohibit these "dangerous" breeds entirely, but do impose strict requirements on the dog owners similar to those imposed on other dogs that are declared dangerous following a hearing, as discussed above.

INSURANCE COVERAGE FOR CERTAIN DOG BREEDS

The insurance industry has begun to re-evaluate insurance coverage for homeowners who own certain dog breeds, such as Pit Bulls, Doberman Pinchers, German Shepherds and Rotweillers. The reason certain breeds are being targeted as higher insurance risks is due to the incidence of dog bites among these breeds.

According to recent statistics, one-third of all homeowner liability claims arise out of dog bite incidents. According to the Insurance Information Institute (III), there were 4.7 million dog bites reported to authorities in 1999, up from 4.5 million in 1996. Most dog bite victims were children.

Thus, homeowners with dogs who are considered high risk may find that they are unable to obtain coverage for liability if their dog bites someone. Unfortunately, this has resulted in an increase in surrender of those dog breeds that are considered high risk to animal shelters.

The Humane Society of the United States (HSUS) is compiling information and statistics on what it calls breed-specific discrimination in homeowner's insurance. If you have experienced breed discrimination as it relates to your homeowner's insurance policy, the HSUS requests that you complete and return a breed discrimination report for their study. More information concerning the HSUS efforts to prevent breed discrimination may be obtained from the HSUS at the following address:

The Humane Society of the United States
2100 L Street NW
Washington, DC 20037

Attn: Companion Animals

A copy of the HSUS Breed-Specific Homeowner's Discrimination Report is set forth at Appendix 2 of this almanac.

CHAPTER 5:
TRAVELING WITH YOUR PET

IN GENERAL

Most experts and animal welfare organizations agree that the preferred way of traveling with your pet is by car. However, there are times when this is not possible, either because you are traveling too far to drive, permanently relocating, or you have limited time to get to your destination. This chapter focuses on air travel with pets, what you can expect, the risks, and the regulations imposed by major airlines.

BE PREPARED

Air travel can be particularly stressful, especially in light of the tragedy of September 11, 2001, and the stringent regulations that have necessarily been imposed on the airlines and their passengers. Traveling with a pet can only add to that stressful situation. Therefore, it is advisable to check with the airlines well in advance of travel regarding any rules and regulations that may apply to air travel with a pet.

According to the American Society for Prevention of Cruelty to Animals (ASPCA), following are their top ten tips for safe air travel with your pet on commercial airlines:

1. Make an appointment with your pet's veterinarian for a check-up, and make sure all vaccinations are up-to-date. Obtain a health certificate from your veterinarian dated within 10 days of departure.

2. Make sure your pet is wearing a collar and an identification tag. Breakaway collars are best for cats. The collar should also include destination information in case your pet escapes.

3. Book a direct flight whenever possible. This will decrease the chances that your pet is left on the tarmac during extreme weather conditions or mishandled by baggage personnel.

4. Purchase a USDA-approved shipping crate that is large enough for your pet to stand, sit and turn around in comfortably. Shipping crates can be purchased from many pet supply stores and airlines.

5. Write the words "Live Animal" in letters at least one inch tall on top of and at least one side of the crate. Use arrows to prominently indicate the upright position of the crate. On the top of the crate, write the name, address and telephone number of your pet's destination point, and whether you will be accompanying him or if someone else is picking him up. Make sure that the door is securely closed, but not locked, so that airline personnel can open it in case of an emergency. Line the crate bottom with some type of bedding—shredded paper or towels—to absorb accidents.

6. Affix a current photograph of your pet to the top of the crate for identification purposes. Should your pet escape from the carrier, this could be a lifesaver. You should also carry a photograph of your pet.

7. The night before you leave, make sure you've frozen a small dish or tray of water for your pet. This way, it can't spill during loading, and will melt by the time he's thirsty. Tape a small pouch, preferably cloth, of dried food outside the crate. Airline personnel will be able to feed your pet in case he gets hungry on long-distance flights or a layover.

8. Tranquilizing your pet is generally not recommended, as it could hamper his breathing. Check with your veterinarian first.

9. Tell every airline employee you encounter, on the ground and in the air, that you are traveling with a pet in the cargo hold. This way, they'll be ready if any additional considerations or attention is needed.

10. If the plane is delayed, or if you have any concerns about the welfare of your pet, insist that airline personnel check the animal whenever feasible. In certain situations, removing the animal from the cargo hold and deplaning may be warranted.

RISKS

There are considerable risks associated with flying your pet on a commercial airline. If your pet is not small enough to fit under your seat, it will usually have to be checked in as cargo, where there is a risk that the animal could be injured, lost or killed during the flight. An animal is considered "baggage." Oftentimes "baggage" gets misdirected or lost. Your precious pet could be getting thrown around on a luggage carousel or sitting in some holding bin at the wrong airport for an extended period of time, with nobody to attend to its needs.

There have also been reports of dogs escaping from their cages while still on the ground, or cages getting crushed during transport. Further, if your plane is delayed, your pet has to suffer in the cargo bin, which may become unbearably hot and uncomfortable. Therefore, if you have no other choice but to fly with your pet, consider the shipping policies of the particular airline. In general, airlines offer three alternatives:

Passenger Cabin

Small dogs may be entitled to ride in the passenger cabin with you provided the pet carrier can fit under the airline seat. Check with the airline regarding size and weight requirements for your pet and the pet carrier. Most airlines charge a fee for this service, however, it is well worth it. This is the preferred method of transporting your pet.

Excess Baggage

Your dog may be able to travel as "excess baggage" if it is within the size and weight limits the airline regularly imposes on excess baggage. However, some airlines refuse to transport certain breeds of dog. If your pet travels in excess baggage, it will ride in a pressurized cargo compartment. However, your dog must be healthy and vaccinated against rabies in order to travel as excess baggage. The airline may require a certificate from your veterinarian; therefore, it is advisable to check with the airline first to determine its requirements. Most airlines charge a fee for this service.

Cargo

If your dog exceeds the size and weight limit for excess baggage, it must be shipped as cargo, the least preferred method of transport. The reader is advised to check with the particular airline to determine the fees and regulations for shipping their dog as cargo.

A summary of airline shipping policies for dogs is set forth at Appendix 3 of this almanac.

The Safe Air Transport For Animals Act

On June 15, 2005, regulations under the "Safe Air Transport for Animals Act" took effect. The Act includes a reporting requirement which provides that all commercial airlines in the United States must report incidents where family-owned pets have been injured, lost, or killed while flying in the cargo hold of domestic flights. The airlines are also required to investigate the circumstances surrounding the incident, and take all necessary remedial action to prevent or minimize such an occurrence in the future. This will give pet owners information necessary to decide which airline poses the least risk of injury to the animal when deciding to travel with their pet. In addition, the Act requires airlines to establish a tracking database for animals in the cargo hold separate from the usual lost baggage claim system.

The ASPCA introduced the bill and was instrumental in its passage, acting in response to the airline industry's annual estimate of 5,000 animals injured, lost, or killed during transport in the late 1990s. Nevertheless, because of strong opposition from the airline industry, an important provision of the Act calling for new cargo holds that are not only pressurized, but also temperature-controlled and ventilated was eliminated from the bill. Therefore, the ASPCA warns pet owners that "air travel [for a pet] is no safer today than it was before passage of the law."

A table of pet deaths/injuries/losses by airline (January 2006 – March 2006) is set forth at Appendix 4 of this almanac.

AIRLINE LIABILITY

As stated above, pets are considered "baggage" when traveling on an airline, and every airline ticket sets forth the airline's liability limitations for lost or damaged baggage. Generally, the airline's liability for loss, delay or damage to a passenger's baggage is limited to the minimum required by law—$2,800 per passenger on domestic flights—unless the passenger paid the cost of declaring a higher value for their baggage. For example, United Airline's Baggage Liability clause reads as follows:

BAGGAGE LIABILITY

International

For those international travels, including the domestic portions, subject to the Warsaw Convention, the liability limit for delay, damage or loss is approximately $9.07 per pound ($20.00 per kg) for checked baggage and approximately $400 per passenger for unchecked baggage. Where the Montreal Convention applies, the liability of the UA Carrier for the delay, damage or loss to checked and unchecked baggage is limited to 1,000 Special Drawing Rights per passenger.

DOMESTIC

For travel wholly between U.S. points, liability for delay, damage or loss to checked baggage, including carry-on baggage if tendered to the carrier's in-flight personnel for storage or otherwise delivered into the custody of the carrier, is limited to a maximum of $2,800 per passenger.

For both international and domestic travel, liability for loss, delay or damage to baggage is limited unless a higher value is declared in advance and additional charges are paid. Excess valuation may be declared on certain types of articles. Some carriers, including United, assume no liability for fragile, valuable or perishable articles. Further information may be obtained from the carrier.

Additional protection can usually be obtained by purchasing insurance from a private company. Such insurance is not affected by any limitation of the carrier's liability under the Warsaw Convention or such special contracts of carriage. For further information, please consult your airline or insurance company representative.

Thus, if you are transporting a valuable show dog worth $7,500, and your dog dies during transport, the airline's liability is limited to $2,800 and, unless you declared the full value of the dog, and paid the additional cost, you will suffer the loss of the difference. In addition, an airline may limit the amount you can declare in excess value. If the amount you can declare does not cover the cost of your pet, you may have to purchase additional coverage from a private insurance company.

Challenging Liability Limits

You may try to challenge an airline's liability limitation in court. Depending on the value of your loss, you may be able to take your case to small claims court, which is a more informal, expeditious procedure than litigation in a higher court, and representation by a lawyer is not necessary.

Whether you can prevail in court against the airline depends on several factors, including (1) whether you were aware of the baggage liability limitation; and (2) whether you were afforded the opportunity to declare a higher value for your pet. The Court will consider whether the baggage liability limitation was clear and conspicuous such that you should have known about it, e.g., whether the clause was printed in easy-to-read language or whether it was hidden in fine print; how much time you had to read the ticket; whether you were an experienced airline traveller, etc. In addition, the airline must give you the opportunity to declare a higher value for your pet, and pay the additional cost.

You must also be prepared to calculate your loss, i.e., you must place a dollar value on the injury to, or loss of, your pet. For example, if your show dog died during transport, you should be able to figure out your actual damages based on other show dogs of comparable value. However, if your pet is simply your beloved companion, it will be much harder to prove any economic damages even though the emotional value is considerable. Although courts are split on whether emotional damages are compensable for a pet, the airline may agree to settle with you to avoid any negative publicity, particularly if their liability is clear and the circumstances surrounding the loss of your pet are particularly egregious.

INTERNATIONAL TRAVEL

If you are taking your pet out of the U.S. mainland, you should be aware of any special rules that apply to travel outside of the United States. As set forth in Chapter 9 regarding pet importation, Hawaii requires that all dogs entering the state be quarantined, at the owner's expense, with an exception for special assistance dogs, such as seeing eye dogs. The required quarantine period—e.g., 5, 30 or 120 days—depends on the dog's rabies vaccination history.

The baggage liability limitations are generally lower on international flights, therefore, it is important to check out your ability to declare a higher value for your pet, or arrange for additional coverage from a private insurance company, well in advance of traveling.

When traveling abroad, you must consider the entry requirements and restrictions of the countries you plan on visiting. If your pet does not require quarantine at the port of entry, then you would generally retrieve your pet along with your luggage at the international baggage claim, and proceed through customs. You must list your pet on the customs declaration card.

As set forth in Chapter 9 regarding pet importation, when re-entering the United States, your pet is subject to the same rules and regulations regarding pet importation as if the pet was entering the country for the first time.

CHAPTER 6:
PET HEALTH ISSUES

IN GENERAL

Animals, like humans, get sick. Therefore, it is important for pet owners to be aware of the various types of diseases their pets can carry, and the manner in which germs and infections can be transmitted between pets and their owners.

A table of diseases spread by animals is set forth at Appendix 5 of this almanac.

BIRDS

Different kinds of birds carry different diseases. Depending on a person's age and immune system, there is a chance of contracting an illness from a bird. For example, baby chicks and ducklings carry salmonella bacteria, which is particularly dangerous to children under the age of 5 years old. Following is a list of bird-related diseases and the types of birds who are known to carry these diseases.

Psittacosis

Psittacosis (chlamydia psittaci infection) is a bacterial disease associated with pet birds. It is acquired by inhaling dried secretions from infected birds. The incubation period is 5 to 19 days. Although all birds are susceptible, pet birds, such as parrots, parakeets, macaws, and cockatiels, as well as poultry, are most frequently involved in transmission to humans. The risk groups include bird owners, pet shop employees and veterinarians. The disease causes fever, chills, headache, muscle aches, and a dry cough. Pneumonia is often evident on chest x-ray. Infected birds are often asymptomatic, therefore, diagnosis is difficult. Antibiotics are used to treat the disease.

Cryptococcosis

Cryptococcosis (cryptococcus infection) is a fungal disease associated with wild-bird droppings, including pigeons. When these dried bird droppings are stirred up, this can make dust containing the bacteria travel through the air. People can stir up this dust and then breathe it in when they work, play, or walk in areas where birds have been. Pets, such as dogs and cats, can also get sick from this dust, but people do not get the disease from their pet dogs and cats.

Salmonellosis

Salmonellosis (salmonella infection) is a bacterial disease associated with many birds, especially chickens, baby chicks, ducklings, as well as other animals. It is passed through the feces; therefore, humans can contract the disease by handling these animals. A person's age and health status may affect his or her immune system, increasing the chances of getting sick. People who are more likely to get salmonellosis include infants, children younger than 5 years old, organ transplant patients, people with HIV/AIDS, and people receiving treatment for cancer.

DOGS AND CATS

Dogs and cats can carry diseases, however, it is unlikely that you would catch a disease from your pet dog or cat. There are a variety of bacterial and parasitic diseases your cat or dog can acquire. Some common diseases affecting dogs and/or cats include the following.

Campylobacteriosis

Campylobacteriosis (campylobacter infection) is a bacterial infection associated with cats, dogs and farm animals. Dogs and cats can have this bacterium in their feces, and people who accidentally touch contaminated feces, can get sick. Symptoms of the infection include watery or bloody diarrhea, fever, abdominal cramps, nausea, and vomiting. A rare complication of this infection is Guillain-Barre syndrome, a nervous system disease that occurs approximately two weeks after the initial illness develops. The animal does not have to be sick to pass this bacterium to humans. In order to prevent this disease, wash hands thoroughly if you come in contact with your pet's feces. If your dog or cat has diarrhea, consult your veterinarian.

Cat Scratch Fever

Cat scratch fever (bartonella henselae) is a mild infection caused by a cat bite or scratch that develops at the site of injury. Symptoms include swollen lymph nodes, fever, headache, fatigue, and a poor appetite. Cats with this disease are asymptomatic. Persons with a compromised immune system are more likely to suffer complications from this infection. In order to reduce the likelihood of infection, avoid rough play with cats—especially kittens—and promptly wash any bites or scratches.

Cryptosporidiosis

Cryptosporidiosis (cryptosporidium infection) is a parasitic disease that causes mild to severe infection of the gastrointestinal system including watery diarrhea, fever, abdominal cramps, nausea, and vomiting. Dogs, cats, and other animals can have this parasite in their feces, and people who accidentally touch contaminated feces, can get sick. The animal does not have to be sick to pass this disease to humans. In order to prevent this disease, wash hands thoroughly if you come in contact with your pet's feces. If your dog or cat has diarrhea, consult your veterinarian.

Leptospirosis

Leptospirosis (leptospira infection) is a bacterial disease that can be serious for both humans and animals. In people, the symptoms are often like the flu, but sometimes leptospirosis can develop into a more severe, life-threatening illness with infections in the kidney, liver, brain, lung, and heart. The bacteria are spread through contact with the urine of infected animals. The bacteria can enter the body through skin or mucous membranes, especially if the skin is broken from a cut or scratch. Infected wild and domestic animals may continue to excrete the bacteria into the environment continuously or every once in a while for a few months up to several years.

If your pet has become infected, it most likely came into contact with the bacteria in the environment or through infected animals, e.g., by drinking, swimming, or walking through contaminated water. Common clinical signs reported in dogs include fever, vomiting, abdominal pain, diarrhea, refusal to eat, severe weakness and depression, stiffness, severe muscle pain, or inability to have puppies. Generally younger animals are more seriously affected than older animals.

If you think your dog has contracted leptospirosis, contact your veterinarian immediately. Leptospirosis is treatable with antibiotics. If an animal is treated early, it may recover more rapidly and any organ damage may be less severe. The time between exposure to the bacteria and development of disease is usually 5 to 14 days, but can be as short as a few days or as long as 30 days or more.

To prevent acquiring the infection, do not handle or come in contact with urine, blood, or tissues from your infected pet before it has received proper treatment. In addition, your dog can be vaccinated against leptospirosis, although it is not 100% effective because there are so many strains of the disease.

Rabies

Cats can contract rabies, an extremely serious disease. However, you cannot catch rabies from a properly vaccinated cat. Therefore, the best form of prevention is vaccination, as more fully discussed below.

Toxoplasmosis

Toxoplasmosis (toxoplasma gondii) is an infection caused by a parasite that can be carried by cats and transmitted to the pet owner through the cat's feces, e.g., when the pet owner doesn't properly wash his or her hands after cleaning the cat litter box of an infected cat. To avoid infection, gloves should be worn when cleaning the litter box, and hands should be thoroughly washed promptly thereafter.

Generally, most people's immune systems can easily fight the infection and no treatment is necessary. Pregnant women and people with compromised immune systems are more susceptible to serious illness caused by this disease. For those groups, medications are available to treat toxoplasmosis.

FARM ANIMALS

If you live on, or visit a farm, you should be aware that farm animals, including cows, sheep, pigs, chickens and goats, can transmit a variety of diseases to humans. It is important, therefore, to wash your hands thoroughly with soap and water after having any contact with farm animals. A person's age and immune system affect his or her susceptibility to getting sick from farm animals; therefore, special caution should be exercised by individuals in these groups.

FISH AND AMPHIBIANS

Fish and amphibians, such as frogs and toads, live in water that can contain bacteria. People with compromised immune systems should avoid cleaning out a fish tank due to a bacterium known as mycobacterium that can cause severe illness in this group of people.

HORSES

Although horses can transmit disease to their owners, it is not likely that you will get sick from touching your horse. Contact with bacteria can occur, however, when performing chores such as cleaning the stall due to the likelihood you will come in contact with bacteria in the manure. As described above, campylobacteriosis, cryptosporidiosis, salmonellosis, and leptospirosis are some of the diseases that can be transmitted to humans by horses. In addition, horses can carry rabies, as more fully discussed below.

REPTILES

Reptiles, such as turtles, lizards and snakes, are kept as household pets, and can carry germs that transmit disease to humans. The most common disease transmitted by pet reptiles is salmonellosis, as more fully described above.

POCKET PETS

"Pocket pet" is a term that has been used to describe small pet animals—e.g., hamsters, ferrets, gerbils, mice, and other rodents, etc.—that can literally fit in the owner's pocket. Pocket pets have been associated with the transmission of salmonellosis, as more fully described above. Therefore, in order to prevent disease, it is important to wash your hands thoroughly with soap and water after touching the pet, and any equipment used by the animal. If one animal in a cage at the pet store has diarrhea or appears to be sick, all of the others in that cage may be sick. Therefore, do not purchase any pet from that cage.

Another disease transmitted to humans by rodents is lymphomatic choriomeningitis virus (LCMV). Symptoms include fever, stiff neck, malaise, anorexia, muscle aches, headache, nausea and vomiting, however, not everyone exposed to the virus becomes sick. The disease is transmitted through contact with rodent droppings, urine, saliva, and infected equipment, therefore, it is again important to wash your hands thoroughly with soap and water after handling the pets and keep cages clean, and do not hold the pet close to your face.

RABIES VACCINATIONS

Most states require dog owners to have their pet vaccinated against the rabies virus every year due to the severity of the disease. Rabies is an acute viral disease that attacks the central nervous system of humans and animals. Rabies is a deadly disease, as it is 100% fatal once symptoms appear. Fortunately, if the victim obtains treatment during the incubation period—the time between exposure to the disease and the onset of symptoms—the body is usually able to fight off the deadly virus.

Prevalence

The majority of reported cases of rabies—85% to 90%—involve wild animals, and because wild animals move from place to place, rabies is prevalent throughout the United States, except Hawaii. According to the Centers for Disease Control (CDC), rabies is most prevalent on the East Coast.

The species of animals that carry and spread disease include skunks, raccoons, bats, cats, foxes, cattle, dogs, horses/mules, groundhogs, sheep, goats and swine. In Florida, the worst rabies culprits are raccoons, foxes, and bats. However, unvaccinated or stray domestic animals, such as dogs and cats, present the greatest risk of rabies to humans. Rats, mice, squirrels, hamsters, guinea pigs, gerbils, chipmunks and rabbits are rarely infected with rabies.

Transmission

Rabies is generally transmitted through bites and scratches from animal to animal or animal to human as the infected saliva is passed through the wound in the skin. Rabies can also be passed if the infected animal licks any areas of broken skin on the victim and the saliva enters the victim. Blood and urine do not contain the virus.

Infected wild animals can easily transmit rabies to pets or domestic animals. Horses and cattle are infected when bitten by animals such as skunks, raccoons, or foxes. Humans who come in contact with these animals are then placed at risk. There has never been a reported case of a human catching rabies from another human, although the possibility of human-to-human transmission cannot be ruled out.

Symptoms

In humans, rabies can take up to a year for the symptoms to appear, although symptoms can appear much sooner—e.g., within nine days of exposure. Generally, symptoms appear within 60 days in most people, the earliest of which may include pain or numbness at the wound site; fever; sore throat; nausea; vomiting; diarrhea; abdominal pain, and lethargy.

Early central nervous system symptoms include anxiety, agitation, nervousness, insomnia, depression. Bites to the head and neck area are particularly dangerous due to their proximity to the brain. The symptoms progress very quickly, and include paralysis, throat spasms, delirium, hallucinations, coma, and cardiac arrhythmia, until the victim finally succumbs to the disease.

Treatment

Fortunately, there are not very many cases of human rabies in the United States. However, because the disease is difficult to diagnose due to its complexity and variety of symptoms, any possible exposure, including a lick from a suspicious animal, must be evaluated immediately by a medical professional. Treatment must be initiated as soon after exposure as possible to avoid potentially fatal complications from the infection.

If the animal is dead, you should carefully save the body for examination using protective clothing, including gloves. If the animal is alive, and can be safely captured without further exposure, it can be observed for the disease. If the animal escapes, you should note its description to provide authorities for possible identification. The only definitive testing that can determine whether an animal was truly infected by rabies is a brain tissue test that obviously cannot be performed on a live animal.

Rabies treatment consists of six injections over the course of 30 days—one shot at the site of the bite and the rest in the arm. This treatment has proven to be 100% effective in stopping the infection if administered within the first 14 days of exposure.

Prevention

It is extremely important to have your pet vaccinated against rabies every year, and kept away from wild animals. Dogs should be kept on your property, and on a leash when off of the property. Cats should remain indoors as much as possible. Children should be instructed not to play with any stray animals, including dogs and cats.

It is difficult to identify a rabid animal. Symptoms, such as foaming of the mouth, do not appear until the latter stages of infection, if at all. Therefore, the best way to recognize a rabid animal is to watch its behavior. For example, if a previously passive animal starts acting aggressively, or a wild animal starts to act friendly, this could be a sign that the animal is rabid. Rabid animals may also appear restless or exhibit a change in their barks or growls. If you see an unfamiliar animal exhibiting any abnormal or unusual behavior, extreme caution should be undertaken.

Horse Rabies

Most pet owners are aware of the rabies vaccination requirements for dogs and cats; however, they overlook the fact that a pet horse is also highly susceptible to the rabies disease. In fact, horses may be more at risk than dogs and cats because they are often kept in locations where they may more easily interact with infected wild animal.

A horse that becomes infected with the rabies virus will need to be euthanized to prevent it from suffering an agonizing death. Unlike humans, there is no rabies treatment for horses and other animals. Thus, it is extremely important to have your pet horse, including foals as young as three months, vaccinated yearly against rabies. The vaccines and 12-month booster shots are inexpensive and well worth it. There have been no reported cases of rabies in properly vaccinated horses.

PET HEALTH INSURANCE

Pet health insurance is medical insurance that provides coverage for the health care expenses of domestic pets, such as dogs and cats. Anyone who has had a sick or injured pet knows that veterinary care can be very expensive. Some policies will only cover accidental injuries while other policies cover accidental injuries, illness and well-care visits.

As with other types of insurance, there is generally a deductible and/or co-pay, depending on the policy you choose. The cost of a pet health insurance policy is generally higher for older pets, and some companies may not cover a pet over a certain age. Pet health insurance can be obtained from an insurance carrier offering such insurance. Your veterinarian can also provide information concerning pet health insurance.

CHAPTER 7:
WRONGFUL DEATH OR INJURY TO A PET

IN GENERAL

If your pet is wrongfully injured or killed by a person or another animal, depending on the circumstances, you may be entitled to damages. The wrongful death or injury to your pet may have been an intentional act, or accidental. However, in order for you to recover damages for an unintentional injury to your pet, the other party must have been legally negligent, i.e., their conduct must meet the legal standard of negligence. An increasingly common negligence claim for injury to a pet is veterinary malpractice, as further discussed below.

DAMAGES

If you prevail in a lawsuit for wrongful death or injury to your pet, the most common form of compensation for death or injury to a pet is an award of money damages. These damages may include:

Fair Market Value of the Animal

The fair market value of an animal depends on a number of factors, including the purchase price; the pedigree; age; health; and special value or abilities of the animal, such as a prize-winning show dog. The damages would be calculated as the difference between the animal's market value before the injury less the market value of the animal after the injury. Damages may also include reasonable replacement costs, such as the cost of purchasing an animal of the same breed; cost of licensing, vaccinations and sterilizations, etc.

In addition, some courts have recognized that a pet, such as a dog, is more than just property, and has some additional value—i.e. intrinsic value—to the owner above mere fair market value.

Consequential Damages

Consequential damages are the foreseeable damages that arise from the injury, such as the reasonable costs of veterinary care for the injured animal; medicine, and any other calculable monetary losses resulting from your pet's injury or death.

Punitive Damages

Depending on the circumstances and the laws of the state in which you live, punitive damages may also be available if your pet was wrongfully injured or killed. Punitive damages are awarded in order to punish the offender and deter similar behavior by others. In order to be awarded punitive damages, the defendant's actions must go beyond mere negligence. The actions must be malicious, intentional or in reckless disregard for the safety of the animal and the rights of its owner.

Emotional Distress of the Owner and Loss of Companionship

Another category of damages arises out of a claim for intentional or negligent infliction of emotional distress due to the death or injury of a pet. Damages for compensation for the owner's emotional distress, or loss of companionship, is sought. These are known as non-economic damages. Whether or not you can recover non-economic damages for the loss of your pet depends on laws of the state in which you live.

The reader is advised to check the law of his or her jurisdiction to determine the compensable damages for animal wrongful death or injury cases.

VETERINARY MALPRACTICE

A veterinary malpractice claim involving an animal is similar in nature to a medical malpractice claim involving a human. Basically, the owner must prove the following elements in order to prevail in a veterinary malpractice case:

1. The veterinarian had a duty of care towards the animal, i.e., the veterinarian took on the responsibility of treating the animal.

2. In treating the animal, the veterinarian departed from acceptable standards of veterinary practice. Expert testimony by a veterinarian is usually necessary to demonstrate that the defendant veterinarian's conduct fell below the professional standard of care exercised by other veterinarians in the community, unless the veterinarian's actions were so obviously negligent that a lay jury can impute liability to the defendant without the necessity of expert testimony.

3. The veterinarian's departure from acceptable standards caused the death or injury of the animal.

4. The death or injury of the animal caused the plaintiff owner to suffer damages. Economic and non-economic damages are discussed above.

A sample complaint for veterinary malpractice is set forth at Appendix 6 of this almanac.

The animal's owner must bring the veterinary malpractice case within the state's applicable statute of limitations. Therefore, the reader is advised to check his or her state law to find out whether a veterinary malpractice case has the same statute of limitations as a routine personal injury case, or if it is categorized as a professional malpractice case, in which case it would be subject to a shorter statute of limitations in most jurisdictions.

Although veterinary malpractice cases are not new, recovery is generally limited to replacement value of the animal, i.e., economic damages as previously discussed. This is because an animal is considered property under the law. These cases are routinely brought in small claims court because of the limited monetary recovery. However, animal rights activists have been campaigning, with some success, to change the "property" status of a pet, and recover non-economic and punitive damages for the negligent loss or injury of a pet.

Veterinarians are licensed in the state where they practice and, as professionals, are required to maintain a certain level of professional conduct in their practice. Complaints against a veterinarian for fraud, negligence, incompetence and malpractice can be brought to the state licensing board for investigation. If it is found that the veterinarian did commit the acts alleged in the complaint, his or her license may be suspended or revoked. Although the veterinarian may be punished and deterred from future misconduct, the animal's owner cannot recover any monetary damages by filing a complaint.

CHAPTER 8:
ESTATE PLANNING FOR YOUR PET

IN GENERAL

If you are like many pet owners, your pet is an important member of your family. So, it is understandable that you would want to make sure your pet is well cared for when you are no longer able to do so, due to illness, disability or death. You may informally ask a family member or friend to take care of your pet. If your pet is a fish or a hamster, this may not be such a big favor to ask. However, if your pet is a dog or cat, this can be an expensive and time-consuming task. Larger animals require a lot of attention, often over a longer period of time, even years.

For example, dogs need to be fed, walked, and groomed, and they may need veterinary care if they become sick or injured. Further, you can't leave a dog or cat home alone for any extended period of time without boarding the animal or finding someone to care for the pet while away. Taking proper care of an animal can become a costly undertaking, and the person you have asked to take on this responsibility may not be in a financial position to carry out your request.

LEAVING MONEY TO YOUR PET

You cannot legally leave money to your pet in your will. An animal is considered property under the law, and you can't leave property to property. For example, if you try to leave money to your dog as a beneficiary, the bequest will likely be declared void, and the money will go to the residuary or alternate beneficiary named in your will. If your pet was the only beneficiary named in your will, then your estate will be distributed according to the laws of intestate succession—i.e., to your closest living relatives pursuant to your state's laws of distribution. In the end, your dog may end up in an animal shelter if your next of kin doesn't want to take on the responsibility.

PROVIDING FOR YOUR PET IN YOUR WILL

You may not be able to leave money or property to your pet in your will, but that doesn't mean you can't provide for your pet after you're gone. For example, you can formally bequeath your pet to a family member or friend who has agreed to take on the responsibility. Of course, that person can still refuse the "gift" when the time comes, however, if you have carefully made your choice, and have seriously discussed all of the responsibilities with that person, it is less likely your pet will be abandoned. You should also leave a sum of money in your will, designated for the upkeep of your pet, to the person you have chosen as caretaker.

Further, you should provide for a back-up caretaker for your animal in case there has been a change of circumstances and your first choice is unable to take care of your pet. If you do not make any provisions for your pet in your will, your pet—as your property—will go to the residuary beneficiary named in your will, or to your next of kin if you did not make a will.

If you are unable to find anyone who is willing to care for your pet after you're gone, there are organizations that you can pay to take care of your pet for its lifetime. The cost, however, can be as much as $25,000 or more for lifetime care.

PET TRUSTS

A pet trust is another method of providing for your pet if you are no longer able to care for your pet due to disability or death. Under a pet trust, the person designated to manage the trust—the trustee—would use the money you put into the trust to take care of your pet, according to your written instructions. It is important, however, to check the law of the state in which you live because not all states permit pet trusts.

A list of states that allow pet trusts is set forth at Appendix 7 of this almanac.

The Uniform Trust Code

The Uniform Trust Code is the first national codification of the law of trusts. The National Conference of Commissioners on Uniform State Laws approved the Uniform Trust Code in 2000. The Uniform Trust Code is essentially model legislation that must be enacted by state legislatures to become the governing law in a state. On issues on which states diverge or on which the law is unclear or unknown, the Uniform Trust Code provides a uniform rule.

Section 408 of the Uniform Trust Code addresses trusts that have been created to provide for the care of an animal during the lifetime of the owner—known as the "settlor" of the trust. The trust terminates upon the death of the animal or, if the trust was created to provide for the care of more than one animal alive during the settlor's lifetime, upon the death of the last surviving animal.

The provisions of a pet trust may be enforced by a person appointed in the terms of the trust or, if no person is so appointed, by a person appointed by the court. In addition, a person having an interest in the welfare of the animal may request the court to appoint a person to enforce the trust or to remove a person appointed.

The property of a pet trust may be applied only to its intended use—i.e. care for the animal—however, if the court determines that the value of the trust property exceeds the amount required for the care of the animal, the court can order that the excess be distributed to the settlor's successors in interest. For example, if the trust designates $50,000 a year for the care of one cat, the Court can determine that this amount is excessive, and order that the excess amount be distributed to the settlor's next of kin.

The following states have enacted the Uniform Trust Code, in whole or in part, in their statutes authorizing trusts for animals, including: Arkansas; District of Columbia; Kansas; Maine; Missouri; Nebraska; New Hampshire; New Mexico; Oregon; Rhode Island; South Carolina; Tennessee; Virginia; and Wyoming.

The Uniform Trust Code § 408–Trust for Care of Animal is set forth at Appendix 8 of this almanac.

The Uniform Probate Code § 2-907

Other states that have not enacted the pet trust provisions of the Uniform Trust Code have adopted the Uniform Probate Code § 2-907 in order to authorize the establishment of pet trusts. These states include: Alaska; Arizona; Colorado; Hawaii; Illinois; Michigan; Montana; North Carolina; Utah; Texas; and Washington.

The Uniform Probate Code § 2-907–Honorary Trusts: Trusts for Pets is set forth at Appendix 9 of this almanac.

CHAPTER 9:
IMPORTING A PET TO THE UNITED STATES

IN GENERAL

The importation of animals commonly kept as pets, such as dogs, cats, birds, and fish into the United States is governed by regulations devised by the Centers for Disease Control (CDC), as further discussed below. In addition, any pets that leave the United States are subject to the same regulations when they return as the animals that are entering the United States for the first time.

The CDC does not require general certificates of health for pets entering the United States. However, the particular state you are bringing the pet into, and or the airline on which your pet will be traveling, may require a health certificate. Therefore, the reader is advised to check with the appropriate authorities prior to bringing the animal into the United States.

HEALTH REQUIREMENTS AND VACCINATIONS FOR DOGS AND CATS

Although the CDC does not require a general certificate of health for a pet dog to enter the United States, they are subject to inspection at ports of entry. If there is any evidence that the dog is sick, an examination by a licensed veterinarian, at the owner's expense, will be required at the port of entry.

In addition, a dog must have proof that it has been vaccinated against rabies at least 30 days prior to entry into the United States. If the dog is a puppy, less than three months old and thus too young to be vaccinated, or if the dog does not have proof that it has been vaccinated, it may still be allowed to enter the United States provided the person importing the pet dog completes a confinement agreement and makes sure that all of the terms of the agreement are met.

The Confinement Agreement

The confinement agreement provides that the dog will be confined until it is considered adequately vaccinated against rabies—i.e., 30 days after the date of vaccination. The vaccination must be given within four days of their arriving at their final U.S. destination, and within 10 days of entering the United States. Puppies that are too young to be vaccinated must be confined until they are old enough to be vaccinated and 30 days thereafter. During its confinement period, the dog cannot be sold or transferred to another owner.

A sample CDC Confinement Agreement (CDC 75.37[E]) is set forth at Appendix 10 of this almanac.

An exception to the proof of vaccination requirement exists if the dog is being imported from a country that does not have the rabies virus for a period of six months before the dog is imported. However, once the dog arrives in the United States, it must be vaccinated periodically for rabies as required by state and local law. In addition, all pet dogs arriving in Hawaii or Guam are subject to local quarantine requirements, even if the dog is from the U.S. mainland.

A list of countries with and without reported cases of rabies is set forth at Appendix 11 of this almanac.

As with dogs, the CDC does not require a general health certificate for a pet cat to enter the United States, however, cats are also subject to inspection at ports of entry and if a cat appears sick, it must be examined by a licensed veterinarian. A cat, however, does not require proof that it has been vaccinated against rabies in order to be imported, but once it arrives in the United States, it is subject to any state and local vaccination requirements. In addition, all pet cats arriving in Hawaii or Guam are subject to local quarantine requirements, even if the cat is from the U.S. mainland.

HORSES

There are no CDC regulations regarding importation of a horse into the United States provided the horse is not known to be carrying any diseases that can be transmitted to humans. Nevertheless, the U.S. Department of Agriculture requires various periods of quarantine depending on the country of origin of the horse.

EXOTIC AND ILLEGAL PETS

In General

Most people keep dogs and cats as family pets. Some prefer smaller animals, such as birds, fish, hamsters, and gerbils. However, for a number of reasons, not all animals can be kept legally as pets, and others require special permits. Some animals have special needs that cannot be met by the average pet owner, therefore, the law either bans them as pets or places restrictions on owning such pets, including special licensing requirements. Some animals pose too much of a risk to the public to allow people to keep them as pets, and others pose a risk to native wildlife populations if the owner releases the animals or they escape. In addition, there are certain classes of animals that are in danger of becoming extinct; therefore, they are not allowed to be sold. The illegal smuggling of wildlife, during which the animals often die in transport, endangers their populations further.

Because of these restrictions, it is important to make sure the animal you intend to keep as a pet is legal in the area where you live. You should begin by calling the local government agency responsible for licensing animals. They should be able to give you information on the legal status of your intended pet, or they will direct you to the appropriate government agency. The ASPCA and local animal rescue organizations, animal shelters, humane societies, veterinarians and pet shops may also be helpful. In addition, you may be able to find information about the particular species on the internet.

A list of exotic pets is set forth at Appendix 12 of this almanac.

Bats

Because bats are known to carry diseases that can be transmitted to humans, such as rabies and histoplasmosis, they cannot be imported into the United States as pets.

Birds

In an attempt to prevent the introduction of the Avian Flu into the United States, the CDC and USDA currently restrict birds from countries where the avian influenza H5N1 virus is present in poultry.

A list of countries affected by the CDC and USDA import restrictions on pet birds is set forth at Appendix 13 of this almanac.

In addition, the USDA Animal and Plant Health Inspection Service (APHIS) has the following regulations regarding the importation of pet birds from outside the United States, for personal pleasure and not for resale:

1. The owner must obtain an Import Permit from the USDA;

2. The owner must provide a current health certificate issued by a veterinarian employed by the agency responsible for animal health in the country of origin; and

3. The owner must have the bird quarantined for 30 days, at the owner's expense, in a USDA animal import center.

A sample USDA Import Permit Application (VS 17-129) is set forth at Appendix 14 of this almanac.

If the bird is protected by the Convention on International trade in Endangered Species (CITES) and the Wild Bird Conservation Act of 1992 (WBCA), the U.S. Fish and Wildlife Service has additional regulations as part of an international conservation effort to protect exotic wild birds. The regulations cover most exotic pet birds, including parrots, parakeets, macaws, lories and cockatoos, but exempts the budgerigar, cockatiel and rose-ringed parakeet. Under the WBCA, to import a pet bird of non-U.S. origin into the United States, the owner must have continuously resided outside the United States for at least one year, and is only allowed to import two birds per year, per person.

Monkeys and Nonhuman Primates

Monkeys and nonhuman primates are not allowed to be imported as pets into the United States under any circumstances, although they may be imported for other reasons—e.g., science, exhibition—under strict regulations. This is because there are well-documented health and safety hazards associated with exposure to nonhuman primates, such as the Ebola virus, monkeypox, yellow fever, tuberculosis and other infectious diseases.

Reptiles

The CDC does not regulate the importation of snakes or large turtles, however, turtles with shells measuring less than 4 inches may not be imported for a commercial purpose, e.g. for retail sale. Small turtles were commonly kept as pets until it was discovered that they frequently transmitted salmonella to humans, particularly young children. Nevertheless, individuals may import as many as six small turtles for non-commercial use.

In addition, the U.S. Fish and Wildlife Service has certain regulations regarding the importation of reptiles, including pet fish, into the United States.

Small Mammals and Rodents

Small mammals and rodents commonly kept as pets, such as ferrets, rabbits, hamsters, and guinea pigs are not subject to CDC regulations provided they are not known to be carrying any diseases that can be transmitted to humans, unless the particular animal is subject to a specific embargo, such as a civet, prairie dog, and African rodent, due to the risk of disease transmission. For example, civets are known to carry the SARS virus, and African rodents are known to carry the monkeypox virus.

Nevertheless, even if there are no CDC requirements for importing the animal, state or local regulations may apply—e.g., pet ferrets are not allowed in New York or California. In addition, any animals that carry diseases that pose a risk to domestic or wild animals are subject to U.S. Fish and Wildlife Service regulations. There is an FDA-approved rabies vaccination for pet ferrets, however, it is not required for importation. The vaccination is recommended, however to protect the animal and owner from contracting the rabies virus acquired in the United States.

CHAPTER 10:
ANIMAL WELFARE

ANIMAL CRUELTY LEGISLATION

Historical Background

The first animal anti-cruelty law in the United States dates back to 1641, when the Puritans of the Massachusetts Bay Colony enacted their first legal code, *The Body of Liberties.* The Code was comprised of one hundred "liberties." The ninety-second liberty forbids cruelty to animals under penalty of prosecution.

Although cruelty to animals was also punishable under the common law, there were no statutory provisions preventing animal cruelty—other than these early Puritan laws—until the New York State Legislature enacted its first animal anti-cruelty statute in 1828. By 1921, all jurisdictions had some type of animal anti-cruelty statute on the books. Punishments varied under these laws, but generally included a monetary fine and/or a term of imprisonment. Most statutes defined cruelty to include the following:

1. The unnecessary or cruel torture, mutilation, beating or killing of an animal;

2. The deprivation of necessary sustenance, e.g. food and water, to an impounded animal;

3. The use of an animal for fighting or baiting;

4. The carrying of an animal in or upon any vehicle in a cruel or inhuman manner;

5. The use of dogs for pulling carts, carriages, trucks or other vehicles, for business purposes, without license to do so.

6. Abandonment of a maimed, sick, infirmed or disabled animal.

Nevertheless, most early laws specifically exempted animal experimentation from its cruelty laws provided the experiments were conducted properly under the auspices of a scientific organization, such as a medical college or university.

Modern Day Legislation

Modern day animal anti-cruelty statutes exist in all fifty states, as well as the United States territories. Most jurisdictions provide that any non-human living creature is protected under the statute. Some statutes limit protection to domestic animals, captive animals, and/or warm-blooded animals.

A directory of state anti-cruelty statutes is set forth at Appendix 15 of this almanac.

Animal anti-cruelty statutes generally prohibit cruel treatment as defined in the earlier statutes and acknowledge that animals have certain rights, as further discussed below. Nevertheless, prosecutions under such laws are rare and the penalties are relatively minor, thus, lessening the deterrence factor. Animal rights activists are therefore concerned with strengthening the animal protection laws.

Protected Rights

Currently, most animal anti-cruelty legislation provides the following protections for certain classes of animals.

The Right to Nourishment and Adequate Living Conditions

Most states prohibit the deprivation of necessary sustenance and/or the failure to provide an adequate supply of food, water and shelter to a confined animal. Some states require that confined animals receive adequate exercise, ventilation, light, space and clean living conditions.

The Right to Protection from Abandonment

Most states prohibit an owner or responsible person from abandoning an animal without providing adequately for its care. A minority of states provides that the abandonment must be willful, cruel or intentional to be a violation, or that the abandonment was of a domestic animal, or a dying or disabled animal.

The Right to Protection from Poisoning

Most animal anti-cruelty statutes specifically prohibit the poisoning of an animal to inflict injury or death. Again, depending on the jurisdiction, this protection may be limited to certain categories of animals, e.g. domestic animals, livestock, dogs, etc.

The Right to Humane Transportation

Most animal anti-cruelty statutes specifically require that the transport of animals be humanely undertaken. For example, many statutes specify that animals must have room to both stand and recline during transportation; must be provided adequate food and water; and must not have their feet or legs tied together during transport.

Common violations involve pets who are transported in vehicles. A pet owner is not entitled to transport their animal in a vehicle unless the animal is safely enclosed in the vehicle. If the vehicle is not enclosed, such as a convertible, flat bed truck, or pick-up truck, the animal must be confined in some type of container or cage that is anchored down. These laws are designed to protect the animal from falling or jumping from the vehicle. In general, failure to confine the animal may result in a monetary fine in those jurisdictions that have enacted such legislation.

In addition, animal anti-cruelty statutes usually prohibit an owner from leaving a dog in a parked car without providing adequate ventilation, particularly in hot weather. In such cases, a law enforcement officer is usually permitted to remove the animal from the vehicle and take it to a shelter if the animal appears to be in immediate danger. If the vehicle is locked, an officer is generally permitted to take all steps reasonably necessary to remove the animal, including but not limited to breaking into the vehicle without incurring any civil liability to the owner of the vehicle.

Standard of Proof

Many jurisdictions qualify the manner in which the animal cruelty offense takes place in order to be deemed a violation, such as "willfully," "maliciously," "intentionally," "negligently," or "cruelly." Each qualifier carries with it a different standard of proof that must be met in order to find the offender liable. Some jurisdictions hold offenders strictly liable for an act of animal cruelty without regard to the offender's mental state.

Exemption for Scientific Experimentation

Many modern day anti-cruelty statutes exempt animals used for scientific experimentation from their protection. Forty states and the District of Columbia specifically provide some form of exemption for research. Most laws maintain that such treatment must be carried out in a "humane" manner, however, "painful" treatment is not generally prohibited provided it is "necessary" to the experiment.

Domestic Animals

The animal anti-cruelty legislation is generally applicable to domestic pets. Dogs and cats are by far the most popular household pets, yet they have a long history of exploitation and persecution. This is in large part due to their use in laboratory experimentation. Many states have sought to strengthen their animal theft laws, particularly because so many pet thefts occur for the purpose of resale to laboratories for experimentation purposes.

In addition, overbreeding these animals for sale as pets is a continuing problem that has led to restrictions on commercial breeding in many jurisdictions. Some states have enacted laws that prohibit the sale of puppies under a certain age, or until weaned. In addition, the federal Animal Welfare Act specifically authorized the Secretary of Agriculture to set a minimum sale age for puppies, which was subsequently set at eight weeks of age, also provided the animal is weaned.

Overpopulation has led to the enactment of mandatory sterilization laws in a number of states. To this end, many states and animal welfare groups also provide low-cost spaying or neutering clinics for cat and dog owners. Presently, about 75% of pets are neutered. Some states charge higher licensing fees for animals that are not rendered incapable of reproduction. The cost of spaying and neutering a pet is less than the cost of raising puppies or kittens for one year.

Further, crimes involving abandonment or poisoning of pets are in almost all jurisdictions.

The Horse Protection Act

Many individuals keep horses as pets, particularly in more rural areas. Miniature horses are also growing in popularity, and miniature horse owners are now challenging pet ordinances to allow miniature horses to live in suburban neighborhoods as household pets.

Horses are also bred as racehorses, show horses, and work horses. A practice known as "soring" has led to a number of cruelty complaints and has resulted in specific anti-cruelty legislation involving this practice. "Soring" is a type of show horse abuse whereby a mechanical or chemical agent is applied to the lower leg or hoof of a horse for the purpose of enhancing the animal's gait, i.e., forcing him to throw his front legs up and out.

In response to this practice, the *Horse Protection Act* (HPA) was enacted in 1970, and subsequently amended in 1976. The HPA prohibits horses that have been subjected to "soring" from participating in exhibitions, sales, shows, or auctions. In addition, the HPA prohibits drivers from hauling sored horses across State lines to compete in shows.

Violators of the HPA may be sentenced to up to two years in prison, receive fines of up to $5,000, and be disqualified from showing or exhibiting horses, or selling horses at auction.

The *Horse Protection Act* is set forth at Appendix 16 of this almanac.

Reporting Animal Cruelty

If you suspect a case of animal cruelty, you should contact the organization that exercises jurisdiction over animal cruelty laws in your state. In general, local and state police are required to enforce all state laws, including animal cruelty laws, regardless of whether they are contained in the state's criminal code. If possible, you should provide law enforcement officials with the specific section of the animal cruelty law that has been violated in order to assist them in investigating and prosecuting an animal cruelty complaint.

The American Society for Prevention of Cruelty to Animals (ASPCA)

The American Society for Prevention of Cruelty to Animals (ASPCA) is perhaps the earliest and most recognized organization established to prevent cruelty to animals. The ASPCA was founded in 1866 and currently has over one million supporters. The ASPCA operates an animal hospital, and has a locater service for animal shelters and adoption facilities throughout the United States. Approximately three to four million cats and dogs are adopted from such shelters each year.

THE ANIMAL WELFARE ACT

In 1966, Congress passed the *Animal Welfare Act* (AWA) in order to set standards for the care and treatment of certain animals and protect them from inhumane treatment and neglect. The Act was subsequently amended several times to increase regulations, particularly in connection with animals used for research. The AWA is enforced by the U.S. Department of Agriculture

In general, the AWA requires minimum standards of care for animals that are bred for commercial sale, used in research, transported commercially, or exhibited to the public. The AWA covers warm-blooded animals except those used for food, fiber or agricultural purposes, such as farm animals. The AWA does not regulate care of cold-blooded animals.

The AWA standards apply to animal shelters and pounds that are regulated if they sell dogs or cats to dealers. Pet shops are not generally covered unless they sell exotic animals, or they sell animals to regulated businesses. The standards govern nutrition and water, veterinary care, animal handling, housing and sanitation, and protection from exposure to extreme weather conditions. Individuals who own pets are not subject to the AWA regulations, although pet owners are governed by animal anti-cruelty statutes, as set forth below.

The Animal Welfare Act is set forth at Appendix 17 of this almanac.

ANIMAL RIGHTS

A discussion on animal "rights" inevitably invites inquiry into the source of those rights. Are animals automatically entitled to certain rights, as co-tenants of this planet, which humans are obligated to recognize and respect? Are animal rights merely a gratuitous gesture by humans motivated by a sense of moral responsibility?

Many animal rights supporters believe that human and nonhuman animals are co-dependent, and that our continued existence is very much dependent upon our efforts to respect our environment and preserve plant and animal species.

The bottom line for all animal rights supporters is the importance of compassion and concern for the pain and suffering of non-humans. Today, more and more people are expressing concern for the animal species. Vegetarianism is common, and many people have given up red meat and dairy products.

Publicity concerning the horrific treatment of animals in scientific experimentation has led to a significant public outcry for more humane treatment of laboratory animals. Many citizens were alarmed when the torturous treatment of livestock was brought to light. Many zoos have changed their environment to permit animals to roam freely in a recreation of their natural habitat, rather than live encaged.

Legislative Efforts

Legislation has been enacted which seeks to eliminate or reduce the suffering of animals, e.g., the Animal Welfare Act. However, critics of these laws argue that additional protection must be afforded an animal that goes further than merely calling for "humane" treatment. They argue that laws that are designed to reduce animal suffering and death, to be effective, must have at least the following three features:

1. The laws must prohibit animal exploitation and not merely ban "unnecessary" suffering or promote "humane" treatment.

2. The laws must explicitly recognize that animals have interests that cannot be sacrificed or traded away for mere consequential reasons, i.e., the efficient use and exploitation of the animal.

3. Recognition that animals are entitled to respect and recognition of their rights and interests because they are creatures with inherent

value that exceeds any property rights or interests humans may claim.

Animal Rights Organizations

The movement to recognize that animals are entitled to certain basic legal rights has been embraced by a number of organizations. These groups are known generally as "animal rights" organizations, although their position on many issues concerning animal rights differs greatly.

Although proponents of animal rights have the same basic objective—i.e., to protect living creatures from unnecessary pain and suffering—there is a broad spectrum of opinions among various groups concerning the means to achieve this objective, and whether there is any limit to the rights which should be extended animals.

Therefore, within the overall definition of animal rights organizations, there exist differences among the various movements. The three major distinctions fall under the labels of (1) animal welfare; (2) strict animal rights; and (3) animal liberation.

THE ANIMAL WELFARE MOVEMENT

Although the Animal Welfare movement does, in fact, support rights for animals—e.g., that animals have the "right" not to be mistreated—it basically encompasses mainstream organizations with moderate views, such as the ASPCA and the Humane Society of the United States (HSUS).

The animal welfare movement acknowledges the suffering of nonhumans and attempts to reduce that suffering through "humane" treatment, but its objective is not to eliminate the use and exploitation of animals. For example, an animal welfare proponent is not necessarily a vegetarian, and may see nothing wrong with eating meat. However, the animal welfare proponent would be concerned over whether the slaughter of livestock is undertaken in a humane manner.

Animal welfare proponents, unlike strict animal rights supporters, believe that if there is justification, then certain animal rights may be sacrificed. For example, an animal welfare proponent would likely support a law regulating the number of chickens allowed to be transported in a single crate, because it would effectively reduce animal suffering due to overcrowding. Although transporting more chickens in one shipment may be more economical, such a regulation recognizes that animals are entitled to considerate treatment which must not be ignored merely because it would further a human interest.

Nevertheless, a strict animal rights activist would argue that such a law does not go far enough because it does not deny that an animal is human property, and merely substitutes one form of exploitation with another, i.e. the slaughter and consumption of the animal.

STRICT ANIMAL RIGHTS ACTIVISTS

As set forth above, in its strictest interpretation, animal rights activists hold the most extreme views concerning the rights to be afforded animals. They argue that animal welfare groups do not go far enough in that they continue to promote the exploitation of animals, albeit in a more "humane" manner.

The strict animal rights movement explicitly rejects all exploitation of animals for any purpose whatsoever. Their fundamental principle is that nonhuman animals deserve to live natural lives that are free from harm, abuse, and exploitation perpetrated by humans.

A strict animal rights proponent would most likely be a vegetarian who (1) avoids wearing leather or fur; (2) refuses to purchase products that involve testing on animals or which may harm animals, such as pesticides; (3) protests hunting; and (4) boycotts companies that exploit animals.

The strict animal rights proponent is not merely concerned with the humanity of animal treatment, but argues that animals, like humans, have the right to be free from human cruelty and exploitation. They refer to the practice of withholding such rights to animals based on their species membership as "specieism," and seek to abolish the status of animals as human property.

Animal rights activists try to extend these rights beyond our human species to include other animals, who are also capable of feeling pain, fear, hunger, and thirst. The more extreme element considers forceful or unlawful action a moral imperative in the protection of animals. Actions taken by animal rights activists range from non-threatening legal behavior to unlawful activities, and may include:

1. Sit-ins at companies involved in animal exploitation, and the sabotage and destruction of associated property.

2. Harassment and boycott of companies and/or persons involved in animal exploitation activities; and

3. Infiltration of companies involved in animal exploitation activities.

Some people believe animal rights activists are advocates of violence when it supports their cause. Animal rights proponents counter that their struggle is one of peace, as evidenced by their attempt to reduce animal suffering and death. They argue that this negative portrayal is actually an organized attempt on the part of those who profit from animal exploitation, to scare the public into rejecting the animal rights struggle in favor of the more moderate animal welfare perspective.

THE ANIMAL LIBERATION MOVEMENT

Animal "liberation" is a term used by certain animal rights activists who prefer to compare the movement to gain animal rights to a liberation movement, such as the women's liberation movement. The use of the term "liberation" avoids the commonly encountered resistance among some people who are reluctant to acknowledge that animals are entitled to so-called "rights."

The acknowledged difference between the Animal Liberation movement and the strict Animal Rights movement concerns animal experimentation. Whereas the strict animal rights proponent seeks to end all animal experimentation, the animal liberationists acknowledge that there may be some cases when such experimentation is morally defensible.

A national directory of animal rights organizations is set forth at Appendix 18.

PEOPLE FOR THE ETHICAL TREATMENT OF ANIMALS (PETA)

Perhaps one of the most well-known animal rights organizations is People for the Ethical Treatment of Animals (PETA). PETA is an international nonprofit organization based in Norfolk, Virginia, and the largest animal rights organization in the world. It was founded in 1980 and is dedicated to establishing and protecting the rights of all animals. PETA's position is that animals should not be eaten, worn, nor used for experimentation or entertainment.

PETA works through public education, cruelty investigations, research, animal rescue, legislation, special events, celebrity involvement, and direct action. Among other things, PETA focuses its efforts on ending animal abuse in factory farms, laboratories, the fur trade, and the entertainment industry.

For example, PETA has been responsible for the closure of the largest horse slaughterhouse in the United States. PETA also uncovered abuse in animal experimentation, leading to the precedent-setting Silver Spring monkeys case, which resulted in the first arrest and conviction of an animal experimenter in the United States on charges of cruelty to animals.

PETA was also successful in virtually eradicating animal testing by the cosmetics industry. Through the use of video surveillance and investigations, PETA has uncovered many instances of animal cruelty and has been responsible for the prosecution of many entities under the Animal Welfare Act. As part of its public education and publicity campaign, PETA has also engaged many top recording artists, entertainers, and models in its campaign against furriers, and has successfully crippled this once lucrative industry. They have also educated the student population about their right to seek alternatives to engaging in animal experimentation in the classroom.

APPENDIX 1:
BREEDER COMPLAINT FORM

Please attach all documentation related to this puppy to this form, including breeder papers, medical records, Kennel Club registry papers, legal documents, and anything pertaining to your complaint.

Today's Date: __/__/20__

Breeder Complaint Form
Provided by The Humane Society of the United States

Complainant Contact Information:

Prefix (Ms, Miss, Mrs., Mr.) First Name	Middle Initial	Last Name
Address City	State	Zip Code
Daytime Phone Number	Complete Email Address	

Breeder Contact Information (fill out only if animal was purchased directly from the breeder):

Name   Doing Business As (Name of Kennel/Facility)

Street Address

Phone Number   Website Address (If applicable)

How did the puppy come to your home? (Be specific: air shipped, picked up, driven, etc.)

How did you hear of breeder? (Be specific: Internet (give address), newspaper (please identify paper and date), friend, sign, etc.)

Is Breeder registered with a "kennel club": (American Kennel Club (AKC), United Kennel Club (UKC), Canadian Kennel Club (CKC), other?	Yes	No
Did the breeder provide you with registry papers for your pet?	Yes	No
Did the breeder provide you with medical records for your pet?	Yes	No
Did you sign a contract with the breeder?	Yes	No
Were you advised of any health guarantees on the puppy?	Yes	No
If yes, were they supplied in writing?	Yes	No
Were you advised of any protections afforded to you under state law should the puppy become ill?	Yes	No
Did you request to tour the breeder's home/facility?	Yes	No
If yes, were you provided that tour?	Yes	No

Were there specific concerns you had when touring the facility? Areas you were refused access to? (Please explain)

_____
_____
_____

Pet Store Information (fill out only if animal was purchased at a retail store):

Name of Store	Manager	Sales Person who assisted you	
Address	City	State	Zip Code
Phone Number		Website Address (If applicable)	

Did puppy leave with you the day of purchase?

How did you hear of the pet store? (Be specific: Internet (give address), newspaper (please identify paper and date), friend, sign, etc.)

Did the pet store provide you with transfer documents/breeder papers/other listing the name of the breeder/broker whom the puppy came from?	Yes	No
Did the pet store provide you with kennel club registry papers for your pet?	Yes	No
Did the pet store provide you with medical records for your pet?	Yes	No
Did you sign a contract with the pet store?	Yes	No
Were you advised of any health guarantees on the puppy?	Yes	No
If yes, were they supplied in writing?	Yes	No
Were you advised of any protections afforded to you under state law should the puppy become ill?	Yes	No
Does the pet store also sell exotic animals (fish, birds, rodents)?	Yes	No

Website Information (fill out only if animal was purchased off Internet):

Name	Doing Business As (Name of Kennel/Facility)
Street Address	
Phone Number	Website Address (If applicable)

How did you learn of this specific website?

How was puppy paid for?

How did the puppy come to your home? (Be specific: air shipped, picked up, driven, etc.)

_____

Was there an interview before you were allowed to purchase the puppy?	Yes	No
Did the breeder provide references?	Yes	No
If yes, did you contact those references?	Yes	No
Were you advised of any health guarantees on the puppy?	Yes	No
If yes, were they supplied in writing?	Yes	No

Animal Information:

_____

Type of Animal   Breed   Age when obtained   Sex

Was the animal altered (spayed/neutered) by breeder or pet store? Yes   No
Was the animal altered by you?   Yes   No   If yes, at what age? _____

Please describe the puppy's condition upon arrival/pick up (Use back of page if needed):

_____
_____

Were you advised of veterinary care the animal had received prior to purchase? Yes No
If yes, please explain. Note if information was received verbally or in writing (Be specific: Use the back of this page if necessary):

_____
_____

How soon after purchase did you take the animal to a veterinarian to be examined?

_____

Was it your regular veterinarian or one referred to you by the pet shop/breeder?

_____

Were you required by the pet shop/breeder to use their veterinarian?   Yes   No

Was the vet visit for health exam/vaccinations or because of medical concerns? Please explain (Be specific):

_____
_____

At what point did you first notice the animal may be suffering from medical problems? Please explain (Be specific):

_____
_____

Is the animal currently living?   Yes   No
If no, please explain how he or she died (Be specific):

_____
_____
_____

How old was the animal at the age of death? _____ weeks/months/years

Were there any prior medical conditions that you were aware of upon purchasing the
dog?   Yes   No
If yes, please explain (Be specific):

_____
_____

Did your veterinarian issue a "Not Fit to Sell" certificate upon examining the animal?
Yes   No

Have you contacted any organizations, professionals, or others about your complaint,
besides The Humane Society of the United States?   Yes   No
If yes, please list the agencies contacted:

_____
_____

Have you contacted a lawyer?   Yes   No
If yes, please list lawyers contact information:

_____

Additional Description of Complaint (Be specific. Attach extra pages if necessary):

Print Name	Signature	Date

Please attach all documentation related to this puppy to this form, including breeder papers, medical records, Kennel Club registry papers, legal documents, and anything pertaining to your complaint.

Once this form is complete, make six copies:

Send **one** copy to The Humane Society of the United States, 2100 L Street NW, Washington, DC 20037. (Please include a hard copy of all relevant documents, e.g. medical records, breeder papers, receipts, etc., with this complaint form.)

Send **one** copy to the Department of Agriculture for the state in which the breeder does business.

Send **one** copy **each** to the Attorney General of the state in which the breeder resides and in your state.

Send **one** copy to the Better Business Bureau.

Save **one** copy and all originals for your records.

Contact information for these above agencies should be available in your phone book (state agencies) and on the Internet (federal agencies and Better Business Bureau).

The Humane Society of the United States (HSUS) works towards a humane and sustainable world for all animals, including people, through public education, legislation, and litigation, and is the nation's largest animal protection organization with over eight million members and constituents.

While The HSUS will do what it can to help you resolve your complaint, we cannot promise that an outcome will be what you hope for. The HSUS is not a law enforcement agency, nor a legal firm, but rather an organization dedicated to using its resources to help advance the cause of animal welfare across the globe.

Due to the large volume of breeder complaints received by The HSUS on a daily basis, we cannot guarantee a response within a certain time period, although every effort will be made. In most cases we will be in touch should we require additional information.

APPENDIX 2:
BREED SPECIFIC HOMEOWNER'S DISCRIMINATION REPORT

Breed Specific Homeowner's Discrimination Report   Date_____

Homeowner's Information
Last Name_____ First Name_____
Street Address_____
City_____ State_____ Zip _____
Daytime Phone Number_____ Email Address_____

May we contact you in the future for more information or about additional work we are doing related to dogs and homeowner's insurance? _____
Would you be interested in speaking to the media in the future about your case? _____

Number of adults living in the home _____
Number of children between the ages of 8-12 living in the home. _____
Number of children between the ages of 3-8 living in the home. _____
Number of children under three living in the home. _____

Animal Information (please fill out the information below for <u>each dog who resides in your home</u>.)

Name _____
Breed/Predominant Breed _____
Approximate Weight _____
Reproductive Status (circle one)   Male   Neutered Male   Female   Spayed Female
Age _____
How long have you owned the dog?_____

Has your dog been through obedience training? _____
If yes, what kind? _____
Does your dog have a regular veterinarian? _____
If yes, how long with this veterinarian? _____
If not, is there a reason why? _____

Has your dog ever bitten anyone? _____
If yes, was it reported to animal control? _____
Have you ever been cited by Animal Control/Police for problems related to your dog? _____
If yes, what was the reason? _____
_____
Has your dog ever been picked up by Animal Control/Police for running at large? _____
Has their ever been a complaint lodged against this dog from a member of the public? _____
If yes, what for? _____
_____

Where does this dog spend most of his or her time? (Example: Outdoors in a fenced yard, outdoors tethered to a stationary object, indoors in a crate etc.)
_____
_____
_____
_____

<u>**Insurance Company Information**</u>

Your Situation

Were you refused homeowner's insurance or was an existing policy cancelled?
_____

Policies That Were Cancelled (If you were refused insurance please skip to next section.)
Name of Company _____
Years with this company _____
Other types of insurance with this company (auto, life, etc.) _____
Any prior claims related to this or any other dogs? _____
How did company learn of this dog in the home? _____
_____

How were you informed that they would discontinue your insurance and what was the time frame given?
(Example: via letter, policy would cancel in 14 days) _____
_____

Were any efforts made to try and convince the company to allow you to keep your dog(s) and remain insured by
them? (Example: Letters of Reference from veterinarian, dog trainer, Animal Care & Control, paid additional
liability coverage for dog etc.)
_____
_____
_____

Did you contact other companies for coverage? _____
If yes, and you were refused, please fill out information below. _____
If yes, and you gained coverage, with what company? Are there special provisions related to the dog?
_____
_____
_____

Policies that were Refused
Name of Company Applied To _____
Was information on dog breed asked in initial application? _____
What was the reason given for refusal of coverage? _____
_____

Were options given (i.e. additional liability coverage for dog at an additional charge)? _____
_____
_____

**PLEASE BE SURE TO ATTACH ANY DOCUMENTS STATING WHY
THE POLICY IS BEING CANCELLED OR REFUSED**

**** Please Note: This information is being compiled for reference and statistical information <u>only</u> and only as
it relates to our work regarding breed discrimination and homeowner's insurance. Your information <u>will not</u> be
shared without your knowledge and consent. Unfortunately, at this time The HSUS is not able to advocate
individual cases to insurance companies for coverage.****

Return this form and supporting documents to:
The HSUS, 2100 L Street, NW Washington, DC 20037; Attn. Stephanie Shain, Companion Animals

APPENDIX 3:
AIRLINE SHIPPING POLICIES FOR DOGS

CARRIER	ALLOWS SMALL PETS IN CABIN	ALLOWS PETS AS EXCESS BAGGAGE	FEE FOR BAGGAGE	ALLOWS PETS AS CARGO
AMERICAN AIRLINES	Yes—$80 each way	Yes* (restrictions apply)	$100 each way	Yes. Cost varies depending on size of kennel and distance
AMERICA WEST AIRLINES	Yes—$80 each way	No	N/A	No
CONTINENTAL AIRLINES**	Yes—$80 each way	No	N/A	Yes. Cost varies depending on size of kennel and distance
DELTA AIRLINES	Yes—$50 each way	Yes***	$75 each way	Yes. Cost varies depending on size of kennel and distance
JETBLUE AIRWAYS	Yes—$50 each way	No	N/A	No
NORTH-WEST AIRLINES	Yes—$80 each way	Yes****	Varies	Yes. Cost varies depending on size of kennel and distance
SOUTHWEST AIRLINES	No	No	N/A	No

CARRIER	ALLOWS SMALL PETS IN CABIN	ALLOWS PETS AS EXCESS BAGGAGE	FEE FOR BAGGAGE	ALLOWS PETS AS CARGO
UNITED AIRLINES	Yes—$80 each way	Yes	$100 for small/medium kennels; $200 for large each way	Yes. Cost varies depending on size of kennel and distance
U.S. AIRWAYS	Yes—$80 each way	No	N/A	No

*Federal regulations prohibit shipping live animals as excess baggage or cargo if an animal will be exposed to temperatures that are not between 45-85 degrees F. for more than four hours during departure, arrival, or while making connections. Health certificates dated within 10 days of departure are required for all animals.

** Continental Airlines will accept American Pit Bull Terrier puppies that are between 8 weeks and 6 months of age provided that they do not weigh more than 20 lbs. All other American Pit Bull Terriers will be refused. This embargo does not apply to American Staffordshire Terriers, Staffordshire Bull Terriers, or Miniature Bull Terriers. Crossbreeds with American Pit Bull Terriers are also excluded from the embargo. Continental Airlines has also embargoed the transport of French Bulldogs, English Bulldogs and Bulldogs from May 15 – Sept. 15, 2005 due to the breeds' susceptibility to high heat, high humidity and stress.

***Pets cannot be checked as baggage on Delta flights between May 15 and September 15. Delta will not accept Pug or snub-nosed dogs as checked baggage or as air cargo at any time if the temperature on any part of their trip exceeds 70 degrees Fahrenheit.

**** Northwest Airlines does not accept pets as checked baggage between June 1 and September 15 to/from the following locations: Arkansas, Arizona, Florida, Louisiana, Mississippi, Nevada, and Texas. Federal regulations apply to other destinations.

All policies current as of September 2005.

Source: The American Kennel Club (AKC)

APPENDIX 4:
TABLE OF PET DEATHS/INJURIES/LOSSES, BY AIRLINE (JANUARY–MARCH 2006)

AIRLINE	DEATHS	INJURIES	LOST	TOTAL
Alaska Airlines	0	0	0	0
American Airlines	0	0	0	0
Comair	0	0	0	0
Continental Airlines	1 (heart/lung)	1 (self-inflicted)	0	2
Delta Airlines	1 (unknown cause)	0	1 (improper crate)	2
Frontier Airlines	0	0	0	0
Hawaiian Airlines	0	0	0	0
Horizon Air (5/05-9/05)	0	1 (unknown cause)	0	1
Midwest Airlines	0	0	0	0
Northwest Airlines	0	0	0	0,
Pinnacle Airlines	1 (natural causes)	0	0	1
Skywest Airlines	0	0	0	0
United Airlines	0	0	0	0
U.S. Airways (5/05-9/05)	1 (unknown cause)	1 (improper handling)	1 (improper crate)	13

Source: American Society for Prevention of Cruelty to Animals (ASPCA)

APPENDIX 5:
TABLE OF DISEASES SPREAD BY ANIMALS

DISEASE	SCIENTIFIC NAME	DESCRIPTION
BSE, a/k/a Mad Cow Diseas	Bovine spongiform encephalopathy	An infectious disease associated with cattle.
Brucellosis	Brucella spp.	A bacterial disease associated with farm animals and dogs.
Campylobacteriosis	Campylobacter spp.	A bacterial disease associated with cats, dogs, farm animals, and improper food preparation.
Cat Scratch Disease, a/k/a Cat Scratch Fever	Bartonella henselae	A bacterial disease associated with cat scratches and bites.
Cryptococcosis	Cryptococcus spp.	A fungal disease associated with wild birds, especially pigeon droppings.
Cryptosporidiosis	Cryptosporidium spp.	A parasitic disease associated with cats, dogs, and farm animals.
Escherichia Coli	O157:H7	A bacterial disease associated with cattle and improper food preparation.
Giardiasis	Giardia lamblia	A parasitic disease associated with various animals and water.

DISEASE	SCIENTIFIC NAME	DESCRIPTION
Hantavirus	Hantavirus Pulmo- nary Syndrome	A rare viral disease associated with wild mice.
Herpes B	Herpesvirus 1	A viral disease associated with Macaque monkeys.
Histoplasmosis	Histoplasma spp.	A fungal disease associated with bat guano stool.
Hookworm A	ncylostoma caninum, Ancylostoma braziliense, Uncinaria stenocephals,	A parasitic disease associated with dogs and their environment.
Leishmaniasis	Leishmania spp.	A parasitic disease associated with dogs and sand flies.
Leptospirosis	Leptospira spp.	A bacterial disease associated with livestock, dogs, rodents, wildlife, and contaminated water.
Lyme Disease	Borrelia burgdorferi Infection	A bacterial disease associated with dogs and ticks.
Lymphocytic Choriomeningitis	N/A	A viral disease associated with rodents such as rats, guinea pigs, and house mice.
Monkeypox	N/A	A viral disease recently sus- pected to be associated with prairie dogs, Gambian rats, and rabbits.
Plague	Yersinia pestis	A rare bacterial disease asso- ciated with wild rodents, cats, and fleas.
Psittacosis	Chlamydia psittaci	A bacterial disease associated with pet birds, including par- rots and parakeets.

DISEASE	SCIENTIFIC NAME	DESCRIPTION
Q Fever	Coxiella burnetti	A bacterial disease associated with cattle, sheep, goats, dogs,and cats.
Rabies		A viral disease associated with mammals, including dogs, cats, horses, and wildlife.
Raccoon Roundworm Infection	Baylisascaris procyonis	A parasitic disease associated with raccoons.
Ringworm	Microsporum spp. and Trichophyton spp.	A fungal disease associated with mammals including dogs, cats, horses, and farm animals.
Rocky Mountain Spotted Fever	Rickettsia rickettsii	A ricketssial disease associated with dogs and ticks.
Roundworm	Toxocara canis, T. cati, and Toxocaris leonina	A parasitic disease associated with cats, dogs, and their environment
Salmonellosis	Salmonella spp.	A bacterial disease associated with reptiles, birds, dogs, cats, horses, farm animals, and improper food preparation.
Tapeworm Infection	Dipylidium caninum	A parasite associated with flea infections in cats and dogs.
Toxoplasmosis	Toxoplasma gondii	A parasitic disease associated with cats and their environment.
Tuberculosis, a/k/a TB	Mycobacterium tuberculosis	A bacterial disease associated with deer, elk, bison, and cattle.
Tularemia	Francisella tularensis	A bacterial disease associated with sheep and wildlife, especially rodents and rabbits.

DISEASE	SCIENTIFIC NAME	DESCRIPTION
West Nile Virus	N/A	A viral disease spread by mosquitoes which can affect birds, horses,and other mammals.
Yersiniosis	Yersinia enterocolitica	A bacterial disease associated with dogs, cats, and farm animals. Also associated with improper preparation of chitterlings.

APPENDIX 6:
SAMPLE VETERINARY MALPRACTICE COMPLAINT

CAPTION OF CASE

COMPLAINT

The Plaintiff [name and address] as and for her Complaint, alleges as follows:

FIRST CAUSE OF ACTION—VETERINARY MALPRACTICE - NEGLIGENCE

1. At all times herein mentioned, Plaintiff was the lawful custodian of a domesticated animal, to wit: a two-year-old female golden retriever known as [dog's name]. Plaintiff is a resident of [state/county/town] and a member of the public who was solicited by the Defendant to provide services to the Plaintiff.

2. At all times herein mentioned, Defendant [name of veterinarian] was and is believed to be a veterinarian duly licensed to practice veterinarian medicine and surgery in the [name of state] with offices located at [address], and said Defendant has held himself out to the public generally throughout the state of [name of state] and to the Plaintiff as being qualified and skilled in the practice of veterinarian medicine as possessing and exercising that degree of skill, ability and learning ordinarily possessed and exercised by other skillful veterinarians in the community.

3. On or about [date], Plaintiff consulted Defendant for the purpose of obtaining diagnosis and treatment of the [dog name] and Plaintiff employed Defendant to care for and treat [dog name] and do all acts necessary for the dog's care and treatment.

4. On or about [date], for valuable consideration given, Defendant agreed and undertook to care for and treat [dog name] and do all acts necessary and proper in connection with such treatment.

5. On or about [date], Defendant so negligently treated and cared for [dog name], that Plaintiff and [dog name] were caused to and did suffer the injuries and damages hereinafter alleged, including the dog's demise. In so acting, Defendant failed to use the degree of skill and learning ordinarily possessed and exercised by other skillful veterinarians in the care and treatment of dogs in the community.

6. Further, on or about [date], Defendant negligently and carelessly engaged in a surgical sterilization procedure on [dog name] in such manner as created a risk to the dog's life and which did, in fact, result in injury and death to the dog.

7. On or about [date], Plaintiff became aware that [dog name] had been improperly cared for by Defendant, and [dog name] died as a result of said improper care.

8. [Dog name], killed by and through the conduct of the Defendant had a peculiar and special value to Plaintiff in that said dog had been Plaintiff's constant companion and a loving and respected member of Plaintiff's family for seven years.

9. As a direct and proximate result of said conduct of Defendant, [dog name] suffered severe bodily injury, pain and death requiring subsequent medical attention, as well as attention from the Plaintiff. Said injuries, being permanent in nature and due to said dog's intrinsic value, exceed the minimum jurisdictional amount of this Court.

10. As a further direct and proximate result of the conduct of the Defendant, Plaintiff has incurred veterinarian and related expenses in the sum of [dollar amount].

11. As a further direct and proximate result of the conduct of Defendant, Plaintiff has suffered great emotional and mental pain and suffering due to the death of [dog name], all to Plaintiff's damage in an amount in excess of the minimum jurisdictional requirements of this Court.

SECOND CAUSE OF ACTION—NEGLIGENT INFLICTION OF EMOTIONAL DISTRESS

12. Plaintiff reiterates, realleges and incorporates paragraphs 1 through 11 above, as if set forth in their entirety herein.

13. On or about [date], Defendant so negligently and carelessly treated and cared for [dog name] while said dog was in his care and posses-

sion as to cause [dog name] great bodily injury, physical pain, suffering and death.

14. Given the peculiar, special and sentimental value of [dog name] to Plaintiff, it was reasonably foreseeable that Plaintiff would suffer great mental distress and pain and suffering as a result of the tortuous conduct of Defendant.

THIRD CAUSE OF ACTION—PUNITIVE DAMAGES

15. Plaintiff reiterates, realleges and incorporates paragraphs 12 through 14 above, as if set forth in their entirety herein.

16. On or about [date], Defendant recklessly and wantonly handled, cared for and treated [dog name] by performing surgery and injuring [dog name] and then returning [dog name] in an injured condition without notice to Plaintiff such that Defendant's conduct is believed by Plaintiff to have been fraudulent and malicious, thus not providing Plaintiff with the opportunity to obtain medical treatment for said dog and possibly preventing her demise. Said conduct of Defendant was in either intentional and/or reckless and wanton disregard of the possible consequences to Plaintiff and said dog, and Defendant knew or should have known that said conduct would cause [dog name] serious physical harm and death.

17. The aforesaid conduct of Defendant was intentional and/or wanton and reckless so as to be malicious, fraudulent and Defendant knew or should have known of the possibility of harm to [dog name] and to Plaintiff. Plaintiff is seeking damages in an amount in excess of the minimum jurisdictional requirements of this Court.

18. Plaintiff requests a jury trial.

WHEREFORE, Plaintiff demands judgment against the Defendant as follows:

1. General compensatory damages according to the proof.

2. Veterinary and related expenses according to the proof.

3. Damages for emotional distress, pain and suffering.

4. Punitive and exemplary damages.

5. Attorney's fees and costs.

6. Any other relief this Court deems appropriate.

Signature Line: Plaintiff or Plaintiff's Attorney/Address/Telephone

APPENDIX 7:
STATES THAT ALLOW PET TRUSTS

Alaska
Arizona
Arkansas
California
Colorado
District of Columbia
Florida
Hawaii
Idaho
Illinois
Iowa
Kansas
Maine
Michigan
Missouri
Montana
Nebraska
Nevada
New Hampshire
New Jersey
New Mexico
New York
North Carolina
Oregon
Tennessee
Texas
Utah
Washington
Wisconsin
Wyoming

APPENDIX 8:
UNIFORM TRUST CODE § 408—TRUST
FOR CARE OF ANIMAL

STATE LAWS

SECTION 408.

TRUST FOR CARE OF ANIMAL.

Last Revised or Amended in 2003

Drafted by the NATIONAL CONFERENCE OF COMMISSIONERS ON
UNIFORM LAWS

(a) A trust may be created to provide for the care of an animal alive
during the settlor's lifetime. The trust terminates upon the death of
the animal or, if the trust was created to provide for the care of more
than one animal alive during the settlor's lifetime, upon the death of
the last surviving animal.

(b) A trust authorized by this section may be enforced by a person appointed in the terms of the trust or, if no person is so appointed, by a
person appointed by the court. A person having an interest in the
welfare of the animal may request the court to appoint a person to
enforce the trust or to remove a person appointed.

(c) Property of a trust authorized by this section may be applied only
to its intended use, except to the extent the court determines that the
value of the trust property exceeds the amount required for the intended use. Except as otherwise provided in the terms of the trust,
property not required for the intended use must be distributed to the
settlor, if then living, otherwise to the settlor's successors in interest.

Comment

This section and the next section of the Code validate so called honorary trusts. Unlike honorary trusts created pursuant to the common law of trusts, which are arguably no more than powers of appointment, the trusts created by this and the next section are valid and enforceable. For a discussion of the common law doctrine, see Restatement (Third) of Trusts Section 47 (Tentative Draft No. 2, approved 1999); Restatement (Second) of Trusts Section 124 (1959).

This section addresses a particular type of honorary trust, the trust for the care of an animal. Section 409 specifies the requirements for trusts without ascertainable beneficiaries that are created for other noncharitable purposes. A trust for the care of an animal may last for the life of the animal. While the animal will ordinarily be alive on the date the trust is created, an animal may be added as a beneficiary after that date as long as the addition is made prior to the settlor's death. Animals in gestation but not yet born at the time of the trust's creation may also be covered by its terms. A trust authorized by this section may be created to benefit one designated animal or several designated animals.

Subsection (b) addresses enforcement. Noncharitable trusts ordinarily may be enforced by their beneficiaries. Charitable trusts may be enforced by the State's attorney general or by a person deemed to have a special interest. See Restatement (Second) of Trusts Section 391 (1959). But at common law, a trust for the care of an animal or a trust without an ascertainable beneficiary created for a noncharitable purpose was unenforceable because there was no person authorized to enforce the trustee's obligations.

Sections 408 and 409 close this gap. The intended use of a trust authorized by either section may be enforced by a person designated in the terms of the trust or, if none, by a person appointed by the court. In either case, Section 110(b) grants to the person appointed the rights of a qualified beneficiary for the purpose of receiving notices and providing consents. If the trust is created for the care of an animal, a person with an interest in the welfare of the animal has standing to petition for an appointment. The person appointed by the court to enforce the trust should also be a person who has exhibited an interest in the animal's welfare. The concept of granting standing to a person with a demonstrated interest in the animal's welfare is derived from the Uniform Guardianship and Protective Proceedings Act, which allows a person interested in the welfare of a ward or protected person to file petitions on behalf of the ward or protected person. See, e.g., Uniform Probate Code Sections 5-210(b), 5-414(a).

Subsection (c) addresses the problem of excess funds. If the court determines that the trust property exceeds the amount needed for the intended purpose and that the terms of the trust do not direct the disposition, a resulting trust is ordinarily created in the settlor or settlor's successors in interest. See Restatement (Third) of Trusts Section 47 (Tentative Draft No. 2, approved 1999); Restatement (Second) of Trusts Section 124 (1959). Successors in interest include the beneficiaries under the settlor's will, if the settlor has a will, or in the absence of an effective will provision, the settlor's heirs. The settlor may also anticipate the problem of excess funds by directing their disposition in the terms of the trust. The disposition of excess funds is within the settlor's control. See Section 105(a). While a trust for an animal is usually not created until the settlor's death, subsection (a) allows such a trust to be created during the settlor's lifetime. Accordingly, if the settlor is still living, subsection (c) provides for distribution of excess funds to the settlor, and not to the settlor's successors in interest.

Should the means chosen not be particularly efficient, a trust created for the care of an animal can also be terminated by the trustee or court under Section 414. Termination of a trust under that section, however, requires that the trustee or court develop an alternative means for carrying out the trust purposes. See Section 414(c).

This section and the next section are suggested by Section 2-907 of the Uniform Probate Code, but much of this and the following section is new.

APPENDIX 9:
UNIFORM PROBATE CODE §
2-907—HONORARY TRUSTS: TRUSTS FOR PETS

UNIFORM PROBATE CODE § 2-907

§ 2-907. HONORARY TRUSTS; TRUSTS FOR PETS.

(a) [Honorary Trust.] Subject to subsection (c), if (i) a trust is for a specific lawful noncharitable purpose or for lawful noncharitable purposes to be selected by the trustee and (ii) there is no definite or definitely ascertainable beneficiary designated, the trust may be performed by the trustee for [21] years but no longer, whether or not the terms of the trust contemplate a longer duration.

(b) [Trust for Pets.] Subject to this subsection and subsection (c), a trust for the care of a designated domestic or pet animal is valid. The trust terminates when no living animal is covered by the trust. A governing instrument must be liberally construed to bring the transfer within this subsection, to presume against the merely precatory or honorary nature of the disposition, and to carry out the general intent of the transferor. Extrinsic evidence is admissible in determining the transferor's intent.

(c) [Additional Provisions Applicable to Honorary Trusts and Trusts for Pets.] In addition to the provisions of subsection (a) or (b), a trust covered by either of those subsections is subject to the following provisions:

(1) Except as expressly provided otherwise in the trust instrument, no portion of the principal or income may be converted to the use of the trustee or to any use other than for the trust's purposes or for the benefit of a covered animal.

(2) Upon termination, the trustee shall transfer the unexpended trust property in the following order:

(i) as directed in the trust instrument;

(ii) if the trust was created in a nonresiduary clause in the transferor's will or in a codicil to the transferor's will, under the residuary clause in the transferor's will; and

(iii) if no taker is produced by the application of subparagraph (i) or (ii), to the transferor's heirs under Section 2-711.

(3) For the purposes of Section 2-707, the residuary clause is treated as creating a future interest under the terms of a trust.

(4) The intended use of the principal or income can be enforced by an individual designated for that purpose in the trust instrument or, if none, by an individual appointed by a court upon application to it by an individual.

(5) Except as ordered by the court or required by the trust instrument, no filing, report, registration, periodic accounting, separate maintenance of funds, appointment, or fee is required by reason of the existence of the fiduciary relationship of the trustee.

(6) A court may reduce the amount of the property transferred, if it determines that that amount substantially exceeds the amount required for the intended use. The amount of the reduction, if any, passes as unexpended trust property under subsection (c)(2).

(7) If no trustee is designated or no designated trustee is willing or able to serve, a court shall name a trustee. A court may order the transfer of the property to another trustee, if required to assure that the intended use is carried out and if no successor trustee is designated in the trust instrument or if no designated successor trustee agrees to serve or is able to serve. A court may also make such other orders and determinations as shall be advisable to carry out the intent of the transferor and the purpose of this section.

COMMENT

Subsection (a) of this section authorizes so-called honorary trusts and places a 21-year limit on their duration. The figure "21" is bracketed to indicate that an enacting state may select a different figure.

Subsection (b) provides more elaborate provisions for a particular type of honorary trust, the trust for the care of domestic or pet animals. Under subsection (b), a trust for the care of a designated domestic or pet animal is valid. Subsection (b) meets a concern of many pet owners by providing them a means for leaving funds to be used for the pet's care.

APPENDIX 10
CDC CONFINEMENT AGREEMENT

DEPARTMENT OF HEALTH AND HUMAN SERVICES
PUBLIC HEALTH SERVICE
CENTERS FOR DISEASE CONTROL
ATLANTA, GEORGIA 30333

Reset Form

NOTICE TO OWNERS AND IMPORTERS OF DOGS

(Please print)

POINT OF ENTRY - CITY   DATE

OWNER'S NAME   PASSPORT No.

OWNER'S COMPLETE ADDRESS &, TELEPHONE No.   DRIVER'S LICENSE No.   STATE ISSUED

                                                 ADDRESS WHERE DOG(S) WILL BE CONFINED

The following dog(s) (number, type, age, and description):

which arrived on
(Kind of conveyance - Name of Ship; Flight No. of Plane; Tag No. of Vehicle)

from   , is/are admitted

to the United States, subject to restrictions of section 71.51 of Public Health Service Foreign Quarantine Regulations checked below:

1. ☐ *"Confinement" for ____ days, which will complete a 30 day period from the date of the antirabies vaccination*
   (§ 71.51 (c) (2) (i).)

2. ☐ *"Confinement" until three months of age; then antirabies vaccination to be followed by confinement for 30 days.*
   (§ 71.51 (c) (2) (ii).)

3. ☐ *"Confinement" until antirabies vaccination at destination to be followed by "confinement" for 30 days.*
   (§ 71.51 (c) (2) (iii).)

The above restrictions are imposed under section 71.51 Title 42, Code of Federal Regulations, and compliance is necessary before legal quarantine control of the animal(s) is relinquished.

"Confinement" as used above means "restriction of an animal by the owner or his agent to a building or other enclosure in isolation from other animals and from persons except for contact necessary for its care, or, if it is allowed out of such enclosure, muzzling the animal and keeping it on leash."

NOTICE TO OWNER: You are expected to observe this requirement as a safeguard against the introduction of rabies. A person violating U.S. Foreign Quarantine Regulations which provide for this requirement is a subject to a fine up to $1000 and /or imprisonment up to 1 year.

_____
(Signature of Government Officer)

_____
(Name: Please print or type)

_____
(Title)

Statement to U.S. Government Officer

I certify that I am the owner, or authorized representative of the owner, of the above listed dog(s). I further certify that I acknowledge and will comply with the restrictions checked above. Also, I will be responsible for complying with any additional measures that may be required by health departments or other authority in the State of destination.

Copy sent to:

☐ State health officer in
  state of destination   _____   _____
                                                    (Signature of Owner or Representative)   *(Date)*

☐ U.S. Quarantine Station
  (See reverse side)

CDC 75.37 (E), Rev. 05/2004, CDC Adobe Acrobat 5.0 Electronic Version, 05/2004

Save Data   Print   Email Form   Next Page

U.S. QUARANTINE STATIONS AND DIVISION OF QUARANTINE HEADQUARTERS

MAILING ADDRESS AND TELEPHONE	JURISDICTION
Los Angeles, CA Tom Bradley International Airport 380 World Way, Box N19 Los Angeles, CA 90045 (310) 215-2365	All ports in Southern California, Arizona, Colorado, New Mexico, Texas, Las Vegas-Nevada, and the U.S. Mexico Border.
San Francisco, CA San Francisco International Airport PO Box 280548 SFIA San Francisco, CA 94128-0548 (650) 876-2872	All ports in Northern California, Utah, Wyoming and Nevada (except Las Vegas).
Miami, FL Miami International Airport PO Box 996488 Miami, FL 33299-6488 (305) 526-2910	All ports in Florida, Puerto Rico, and the US Virgin Islands.
Honolulu, HI Honolulu International Airport 300 Rodgers Blvd. Terminal Box #67 Honolulu, HI 96819-1897 (808) 861-8530	All ports in Hawaii, Guam, and Pacific Trust Territories.
Chicago, IL O'Hare International Airport AMC O'Hare, POB 66012 Chicago, IL 60666-0012 (773) 894-2960	All ports in Illinois, Indiana, Iowa, Kansas, Kentucky, Michigan, Minnesota, Missouri, Nebraska, North Dakota, Ohio, South Dakota, and Wisconsin. Canadian pre-clearance port: Toronto.
Jamaica, NY JFK International Airport Room 219.016 Terminal 4(E) Jamaica, NY 11430-1081 (718) 553-1685	All ports in New York, Connecticut, Delaware, District of Columbia, Maine, Maryland, Massachusetts, New Hampshire, New Jersey, Pennsylvania, Rhode Island, Vermont, Virginia, and West Virginia. Canadian pre-clearance port: Montreal. Also, pre-clearance at Shannon and Dublin.
Seattle, WA Seattle-Tacoma International Airport Room S-2067M Seattle, WA 98158-1250 (206) 553-4519	All ports in Washington, Alaska, Idaho, Montana, and Oregon. Canadian pre-clearance ports: Edmonton, Calgary, Vancouver, and Victoria.
Atlanta, GA Hartsfield-Jackson International Airport PO Box 45256 Atlanta, GA 30320 (404) 639-1220	All ports in Georgia, Alabama, Arkansas, Louisiana, Mississippi, North Carolina, South Carolina, and Tennessee, Oklahoma

For Public Health assistance, contact the appropriate office above.

The Centers for Disease Control and Prevention, an agency of the Department of Health and Human Services, is authorized to collect this information under provisions of the Public Health Service Act, Section 301 (42 U.S.C. 241). Response in this case is voluntary and there is no penalty for non-response. The individually identified data may be shared with health departments and other public health authorities used to locate animal owners if the address is invalid.

CDC 75.37 (E), Rev. 05/2004, CDC Adobe Acrobat 5.0 Electronic Version, 05/2004

APPENDIX 11:
COUNTRIES WITH/WITHOUT RABIES DISEASE

COUNTRIES WITH PRESENCE OF RABIES DISEASE

AFRICA

Algeria
Botswana
Central African
Republic Ethiopia
Ghana
Guinea
Kenya
Lesotho
Madagascar
Malawi
Mali
Morocco
Mozambique
Namibia
Nigeria
Senegal
South Africa Sudan
Swaziland
Togo
Tunisia
Uganda
United Republic of Tanzania
Zimbabwe

AMERICAS

Argentina
Belize
Bolivia
Brazil
Canada
Chile
Colombia
Costa Rica
Cuba
Dominican Republic
Ecuador
El Salvador
Guatemala
Guyana
Haiti
Honduras
Mexico
Nicaragua
Panama
Paraguay
Peru
Puerto Rico
Suriname
Trinidad and Tobago
United States of America
Venezuela

ASIA

Bangladesh
Bhutan
Cambodia
China
India
Indonesia
Iran (Islamic Republic of)
Iraq
Israel
Jordan

Kyrgyzstan
Lao P.'s Democratic Republic
Malaysia (peninsular)
Mongolia
Myanmar
Nepal
Oman
Pakistan
Philippines
Sri Lanka
Syrian Arab Republic
Tajikistan
Thailand
Ukraine
Uzbekistan
Viet Nam

EUROPE

Austria
Belgium
Bulgaria
Croatia
Czech Republic
Denmark
Estonia
France
Georgia
Germany
Hungary
Lithuania
Luxembourg
Moldova, Republic of
Netherlands
Poland
Romania
Russian Federation
Slovakia
Slovenia
Spain
Turkey
Yugoslavia

COUNTRIES WITH ABSENCE OF RABIES DISEASE

AFRICA
Cape Verde
Libyan Arab Jamahiriya
Mauritius
Reunion
Sao Tome and Principe
Seychelles

AMERICAS
Antigua and Barbuda
Barbados
Tuvalu
Uruguay

ASIA
Armenia
Cyprus
Hong Kong
Japan
Kuwait
Lebanon
Malaysia (Sabah)
Qatar
Singapore

EUROPE
Albania
Finland
Gibraltar
Greece
Iceland
Ireland
Isle of Man
Italy
Malta
Norway
Portugal
Sweden

Switzerland
United Kingdom of Great Britain

OCEANIA

Australia
Fiji
Kiribati
Micronesia (Federated States of)
Montserrat
New Caledonia
New Zealand
Palau
Samoa
Vanuatu

Source: World Health Organization

APPENDIX 12:
LIST OF EXOTIC PETS

African Clawed Frogs
African Dormice
African Dwarf Clawed Frogs
Alpacas
American Green Tree Frogs
Anoles, Green
Antlions (Doodlebugs)
Aquatic Turtles
Argentinian Black and White Tegu
Asian Water Dragons
Axolotls
Ball Pythons
Bearded Dragons
Blue Tongued Skinks
Boa Constrictor (Red Tailed Boa)
Box Turtles (General info)
Box Turtles, Eastern
Box Turtles, Gulf Coast
Box Turtles, Ornate
Box Turtles, Three Toed
Burmese Pythons
Cats, Non Domestic
Chameleons (General)
Chameleon, Jackson's
Chameleon, Panther
Chameleon, Veiled
Chilean Rose Tarantulas
Chinchillas
Chinese Hamsters
Chinese Water Dragons
Cockroaches, Madagascar Hissing

Corn Snakes
Costa Rican Zebra Tarantula
Crabs, Fiddler
Crabs, Hermit
Curly Hair Tarantulas
Day Geckos
Degus
Desert Blonde Tarantulas
Dormice, African
Dwarf Hamsters (General)
Dwarf Campbells Russian Hamsters
Dwarf Clawed Frogs
Dwarf Winter White Russian Hamsters
Eastern Box Turtles
Emperor Scorpion
Fat-Tailed Geckos
Fennec Foxes
Ferrets
Fiddler Crabs
Fire Bellied Newts
Fire Bellied Toads
Flying Squirrels
Frogs (General Info)
Frogs, African Clawed
Frogs, American Green Tree
Frogs, Dwarf Clawed
Frogs, Northern Leopard
Frogs, Pacman
Frogs, White's Tree
Geckos
Geckos, Day
Geckos, Fat Tailed
Geckos, Leopard
Geckos, Madagascar Ground
Geckos, Tokay
Gerbils
Giant African Land Snails
Giant African Millipedes
Goats
Green Anoles
Green Iguanas

Guinea Pigs
Gulf Coast Box Turtles
Hamsters (general)
Hamsters, Chinese
Hamsters, Dwarf Campbells Russian
Hamsters, Dwarf Winter White Russian
Hamsters, Roborovski
Hamsters, Syrian
Hedgehogs
Hermann's Tortoises
Hermit Crabs
Horsfield's/Russian Tortoise
Iguanas
Insects and Spiders (General Info)
Jackson's Chameleon
King Snakes
Kinkajous
Leopard Geckos
Leopard Tortoises
Leopard Frogs (Northern)
Lizards (General)
Llamas
Madagascar Ground Geckos
Madagascar Hissing Cockroaches
Mantids (praying)
Mexican RedKnee Tarantulas
Mexican Redleg Tarantulas
Mice
Milk Snakes
Millipedes, Giant African
Monitors, Savannah
Northern Leopard Frogs
Opossum, Short Tailed
Oriental Fire Bellied Toads
Ornate Box Turtles
Ornate Horned Frogs (Pacman Frogs)
Pacman Frogs (ornate Horned Frogs)
Panther Chameleon
Pinktoe Tarantulas
Pot Bellied Pigs
Prairie Dogs

Praying Mantid
Primates
Python, Ball
Python, Burmese
Rabbits
Raccoons
Rats
Red Eared Sliders
Red Footed Tortoise
Red Tailed Boas (boa constrictors)
Roborovski Hamsters
Savannah Monitors
Scorpions
Short Tailed Opossum
Skunks
Snails, Giant African
Snakes (General)
Squirrels, Flying
Stick Insects
Sugar Gliders
Sulcata Tortoise
Syrian Hamsters
Tarantulas (General Info)
Tarantulas, Chilean Rose
Tarantulas, Costa Rican Zebra
Tarantulas, Curly Hair
Tarantulas, Desert Blonde
Tarantulas, Mexican Redknee
Tarantulas, Mexican Redleg
Tarantulas, Pinktoe
Tegu, Argentinian Black and White
Three Toed Box Turtles
Tiger Salamander
Toads, Oriental Fire Bellied
Tokay Geckos
Tortoises (General Info)
Tortoises, Hermann's
Tortoises, Horsfield's/Russian
Tortoises, Leopard
Tortoises, Red Footed
Tortoises, Sulcata

Turtles and Tortoises (General Information)
Turtles, Box (also see individual species links above)
Turtles, Red Eared Slider
Veiled Chameleon
Wallaroos
Water Dragons, Chinese
White's Tree Frogs
Wolfdogs

APPENDIX 13:
COUNTRIES AFFECTED BY THE CDC/USDA IMPORT RESTRICTIONS ON PET BIRDS

EAST ASIA AND THE PACIFIC

Burma (Myanmar)
Cambodia
China
Indonesia
Japan
Laos
Malaysia
South Korea
Thailand
Vietnam

SOUTH ASIA

Afghanistan
India
Kazakhstan
Pakistan

EUROPE AND EURASIA

Albania
Azerbaijan
Denmark (USDA—defined restricted zone only)
France (USDA—defined restricted zone only)
Romania
Russia
Sweden (USDA—defined restricted zone only)

Turkey
Ukraine

AFRICA

Burkina Faso
Cameroon
Djibouti
Egypt
Ivory Coast (Cote d'Ivoire)
Niger
Nigeria
Sudan

NEAR EAST

Gaza and West Bank
Israel
Jordan

APPENDIX 14
USDA IMPORT PERMIT APPLICATION

No animals, animal semen, animal embryos, birds, poultry, or hatching eggs may be imported unless a completed application has been received (9 CFR 92 and CFR 93.)

Public reporting burden for this collection of information is estimated to average .17 hours per response, including the time for reviewing instructions, searching existing data sources, gathering and maintaining the data needed, and completing and reviewing the collection of information. Send comments regarding this burden estimate or any other aspect of this collection of information, including suggestions for reducing this burden, to Department of Agriculture, Clearance Officer, OIRM, Room 404-W, Washington, D.C. 20250; and to the Office of Information and Regulatory Affairs, Office of Management and Budget, Washington, D.C. 20503.

FORM APPROVED OMB NO. 0579-0040

U.S. DEPARTMENT OF AGRICULTURE
ANIMAL AND PLANT HEALTH INSPECTION SERVICE
VETERINARY SERVICES
APPLICATION FOR IMPORT OR IN TRANSIT PERMIT
(Animals, Animal Semen, Animal Embryos, Birds, Poultry, or Hatching Eggs)

INSTRUCTIONS TO IMPORTER: Complete and submit one copy to the Veterinary Services, APHIS, U.S. Department of Agriculture, 4700 River Road, Riverdale, MD 20737. Prepare a separate application for each shipment.

1. NAME AND ADDRESS OF SHIPPER IN COUNTRY OF ORIGIN

2. NAME AND ADDRESS OF IMPORTER (Include Area Code)

TELEPHONE NUMBER (Include Area Code)

3. PORT OF EMBARKATION (From Canada show only for ocean vessel or airplane shipments)

4. COUNTRY FROM WHICH SHIPPED

5. MODE OF TRANSPORTATION (Name of Airline or Vessel, flight no.)

6. ANIMALS, ANIMAL SEMEN, ANIMAL EMBRYOS, BIRDS, POULTRY, OR HATCHING EGGS

A. NO.	B. BREED	C. SPECIES	D. DESCRIPTION (Sex, Age, Registered Name and No., Tattoo, Tag No., other Markings)

6E. PURPOSE OF IMPORTATION

7. ROUTE OF TRAVEL INCLUDING ALL CARRIER STOPS ENROUTE (From Canada show route of travel only for ocean vessel or airplane shipment)

8. PROPOSED SHIPPING DATE (From Canada show only for ocean vessel or airplane shipment)

9. PROPOSED ARRIVAL DATE

10. UNITED STATES PORT OF ENTRY

11. NAME AND MAILING ADDRESS OF PERSON TO WHOM DELIVERY WILL BE MADE (After quarantine, when required) (Include Zip Code)

TELEPHONE NUMBER (Include Area Code)

12. WHERE DELIVERY WILL BE MADE IN U.S. (After quarantine, when required) (Location of place)

13. REMARKS

14. SIGNATURE OF IMPORTER

15. DATE SIGNED

VS FORM 17-129 (MAY 96)   Previous edition may be used.

APPENDIX 15:
STATE ANIMAL ANTI-CRUELTY STATUTES

CODE OF ALABAMA 1975 § 13A-11-14 CRUELTY TO ANIMALS.

(a) A person commits the crime of cruelty to animals if, except as otherwise authorized by law, he intentionally or recklessly:

(1) Subjects any animal to cruel mistreatment; or

(2) Subjects any animal in his custody to cruel neglect; or

(3) Kills or injures without good cause any animal belonging to another.

(b) Cruelty to animals is a Class B misdemeanor.

ALASKA STATUTES- § 11.61.140 CRUELTY TO ANIMALS.

(a) A person commits the crime of cruelty to animals if the person

(1) intentionally inflicts severe and prolonged physical pain or suffering on an animal;

(2) recklessly neglects an animal and, as a result of that neglect, causes the death of the animal or causes severe pain or suffering to the animal; or

(3) kills an animal by the use of a decompression chamber.

(b) It is a defense to a prosecution under (a)(1) or (2) of this section that the conduct of the defendant

(1) conformed to accepted veterinary practice;

(2) was part of scientific research governed by accepted standards; or

(3) was necessarily incident to lawful hunting or trapping activities.

(c) In this section, "animal" means a vertebrate living creature not a human being, but does not include fish.

(d) Cruelty to animals is a class A misdemeanor.

ARIZONA REVISED STATUTES–§ 13-2910. CRUELTY TO ANIMALS OR POULTRY; CLASSIFICATION.

A. A person commits cruelty to animals if, except as otherwise authorized by law, such person recklessly:

1. Subjects any animals or poultry under human custody or control to cruel mistreatment; or

2. Subjects any animal or poultry under his custody or control to cruel neglect or abandonment; or

3. Kills any animal or poultry under the custody or control of another without either legal privilege or consent of the owner.

B. It is a defense to subsection A of this section if any person exposes poison to be taken by a dog which has killed or wounded livestock or poison to be taken by predatory animals on premises owned, leased or controlled by him for the purpose of the protection of such person or his livestock or poultry, and the treated property is kept posted by the person who authorized or performed the treatment until such poison has been removed, and such poison is removed by the person exposing the poison after the threat to such person, his livestock or poultry has ceased to exist. The posting required shall be in such manner as to provide adequate warning to persons who enter the property by the point or points of normal entry. The warning notice which is posted shall be of such size that it is readable at a distance of fifty feet, shall contain a poison statement and symbol and shall state the word "Danger" or "Warning".

C. Cruelty to animals or poultry is a class 2 misdemeanor.

ARKANSAS CODE OF 1987–§ 5-62-101 CRUELTY TO ANIMALS.

(a) A person commits the offense of cruelty to animals if, except as authorized by law, he knowingly:

(1) Abandons any animal;

(2) Subjects any animal to cruel mistreatment;

(3) Subjects any animal in his custody to cruel neglect; or

(4) Kills or injures any animal belonging to another without legal privilege or consent of the owner.

(b) Cruelty to animals is a Class A misdemeanor.

CALIFORNIA PENAL CODE–§ 597. CRUELTY TO ANIMALS.

(a) Except as provided in subdivision (c) of this section or Section 599c, every person who maliciously and intentionally maims, mutilates, tortures, or wounds a living animal, or maliciously and intentionally kills an animal, is guilty of an offense punishable by imprisonment in the state prison, or by a fine of not more than twenty thousand dollars ($20,000), or by both the fine and imprisonment, or, alternatively, by imprisonment in the county jail for not more than one year, or by a fine of not more than twenty thousand dollars ($20,000), or by both the fine and imprisonment.

(b) Except as otherwise provided in subdivision (a) or (c), every person who overdrives, overloads, drives when overloaded, overworks, tortures, torments, deprives of necessary sustenance, drink, or shelter, cruelly beats, mutilates, or cruelly kills any animal, or causes or procures any animal to be so overdriven, overloaded, driven when overloaded, overworked, tortured, tormented, deprived of necessary sustenance, drink, shelter, or to be cruelly beaten, mutilated, or cruelly killed; and whoever, having the charge or custody of any animal, either as owner or otherwise, subjects any animal to needless suffering, or inflicts unnecessary cruelty upon the animal, or in any manner abuses any animal, or fails to provide the animal with proper food, drink, or shelter or protection from the weather, or who drives, rides, or otherwise uses the animal when unfit for labor, is, for every such offense, guilty of a crime punishable as a misdemeanor or as a felony or alternatively punishable as a misdemeanor or a felony and by a fine of not more than twenty thousand dollars ($20,000).

(c) Every person who maliciously and intentionally maims, mutilates, or tortures any mammal, bird, reptile, amphibian, or fish as described in subdivision (d), is guilty of an offense punishable by imprisonment in the state prison, or by a fine of not more than twenty thousand dollars ($20,000), or by both the fine and imprisonment, or, alternatively, by imprisonment in the county jail for not more than one year, by a fine of not more than twenty thousand dollars ($20,000), or by both the fine and imprisonment.

(d) Subdivision (c) applies to any mammal, bird, reptile, amphibian, or fish which is a creature described as follows:

(1) Endangered species or threatened species as described in Chapter 1.5 (commencing with Section 2050) of Division 3 of the Fish and Game Code.

(2) Fully protected birds described in Section 3511 of the Fish and Game Code.

(3) Fully protected mammals described in Chapter 8 (commencing with Section 4700) of Part 3 of Division 4 of the Fish and Game Code.

(4) Fully protected reptiles and amphibians described in Chapter 2 (commencing with Section 5050) of Division 5 of the Fish and Game Code.

(5) Fully protected fish as described in Section 5515 of the Fish and Game Code.

This subdivision does not supersede or affect any provisions of law relating to taking of the described species, including, but not limited to, Section 12008 of the Fish and Game Code.

(e) For the purposes of subdivision (c), each act of malicious and intentional maiming, mutilating, or torturing a separate specimen of a creature described in subdivision (d) is a separate offense. If any person is charged with a violation of subdivision (c), the proceedings shall be subject to Section 12157 of the Fish and Game Code.

(f) Upon the conviction of a person charged with a violation of this section by causing or permitting an act of cruelty, as defined in Section 599b, all animals lawfully seized and impounded with respect to the violation by a peace officer, officer of a humane society, or officer of a pound or animal regulation department of a public agency shall be adjudged by the court to be forfeited and shall thereupon be awarded to the impounding officer for proper disposition. A person convicted of a violation of this section by causing or permitting an act of cruelty, as defined in Section 599b, shall be liable to the impounding officer for all costs of impoundment from the time of seizure to the time of proper disposition.

Mandatory seizure or impoundment shall not apply to animals in properly conducted scientific experiments or investigations performed under the authority of the faculty of a regularly incorporated medical college or university of this state.

COLORADO REVISED STATUTES § 18-9-202. CRUELTY TO ANIMALS—NEGLECT OF ANIMALS—OFFENSES.

(1)(a) A person commits cruelty to animals if he knowingly or with criminal negligence overdrives, overloads, overworks, tortures, torments, deprives of necessary sustenance, unnecessarily or cruelly beats, needlessly mutilates, needlessly kills, carries or confines in or upon any vehicles in a cruel or reckless manner, or otherwise mistreats or neglects any animal, or causes or procures it to be done, or, having the charge of custody of any animal, fails to provide it with proper food, drink, or protection from the weather, or abandons it.

(1)(b) Any person who intentionally abandons a dog or cat commits the offense of cruelty to animals.

(2)(a) Cruelty to animals is a class 1 misdemeanor.

(2)(b) In the case of any person incurring a second or subsequent conviction under the provisions of paragraph (a) of this subsection (2), a sentence of imprisonment within the minimum and maximum terms shall be mandatory and shall not be subject to suspension, nor shall such person be eligible for probation or parole for any part of such period. A plea of nolo contendere accepted by the court shall be considered a conviction for the purposes of this section.

(3) Nothing in this part 2 shall be construed to amend or in any manner change the authority of the wildlife commission, as established in title 33, C.R.S., or to prohibit any conduct therein authorized or permitted.

CONNECTICUT GENERAL STATUTES § 53-247. CRUELTY TO ANIMALS. INTENTIONAL KILLING OF POLICE ANIMAL.

(a) Any person who overdrives, drives when overloaded, overworks, tortures, deprives of necessary sustenance, mutilates or cruelly beats or kills or unjustifiably injures any animal, or who, having impounded or confined any animal, fails to give such animal proper care or neglects to cage or restrain any such animal from doing injury to itself or to another animal or fails to supply any such animal with wholesome air, food and water, or unjustifiably administers any poisonous or noxious drug or substance to any domestic animal or unjustifiably exposes any such drug or substance, with intent that the same shall be taken by an animal, or causes it to be done, or, having charge or custody of any animal, inflicts cruelty upon it or fails to provide it with proper food, drink or protection from the weather or abandons it or carries it or causes it to be carried in a cruel manner, or sets on foot, instigates, promotes or carries on or performs any act as assistant, umpire or principal in, or is a witness of, or in any way aids in or engages in the furtherance of, any fight between cocks or other birds, dogs or other animals, premeditated by any person owning, or having custody of, such birds or animals, or fights with or baits, harasses or worries any animal for the purpose of making it perform for amusement, diversion or exhibition, shall be fined not more than one thousand dollars or imprisoned not more than one year or both.

(b) Any person who intentionally kills any animal while such animal is in the performance of its duties under the supervision of a peace officer, as defined in section 53a-3, shall be fined not more than five thousand dollars or imprisoned not more than five years or both.

DELAWARE CODE § 1325 CRUELTY TO ANIMALS; CLASS A MISDEMEANOR; CLASS F FELONY.

(a) For the purpose of this section, the following words and phrases shall include, but not be limited to, the meanings respectively ascribed to them as follows:

(1) "Cruel" includes every act or omission to act whereby unnecessary or unjustifiable physical pain or suffering is caused or permitted.

(2) "Cruel mistreatment" includes any treatment whereby unnecessary or unjustifiable physical pain or suffering is caused or permitted.

(3) "Cruel neglect" includes neglect of an animal, which is under the care and control of the neglector, whereby pain or suffering is caused to the animal or abandonment of any domesticated animal by its owner or custodian.

(4) "Cruelty to animals" includes mistreatment of any animal or neglect of any animal under the care and control of the neglector, whereby unnecessary or unjustifiable physical pain or suffering is caused. By way of example this includes: Unjustifiable beating of an animal; overworking an animal; tormenting an animal; abandonment of an animal; failure to feed properly or give proper shelter or veterinary care to an animal.

(5) "Person" includes any individual, partnership, corporation or association living and/or doing business in the State.

(6) "Abandonment" includes completely forsaking or deserting an animal originally under one's custody without making reasonable arrangements for custody of that animal to be assumed by another person.

(7) "Custody" includes the responsibility for the welfare of an animal subject to one's care and control whether one owns it or not.

(8) "Proper feed" includes providing each animal with daily food and water of sufficient quality and quantity to prevent unnecessary or unjustifiable physical pain or suffering by the animal.

(9) "Proper shelter" includes providing each animal with adequate shelter from the weather elements as required to prevent unnecessary or unjustifiable physical pain or suffering by the animal.

(10) "Proper veterinary care" includes providing each animal with veterinary care sufficient to prevent unnecessary or unjustifiable physical pain or suffering by the animal.

(11) "Animal" shall not include fish, crustacea or molluska.

(12) "Serious injury" shall include any injury to any animal which creates a substantial risk of death, or which causes prolonged impairment of health or prolonged loss or impairment of the function of any bodily organ.

(b) A person is guilty of cruelty to animals when the person intentionally or recklessly:

(1) Subjects any animal to cruel mistreatment; or

(2) Subjects any animal in the person's custody to cruel neglect; or

(3) Kills or injures any animal belonging to another person without legal privilege or consent of the owner; or

(4) Cruelly or unnecessarily kills or injures any animal whether belonging to the actor or another. This section does not apply to the killing of any animal normally or commonly raised as food for human consumption, provided that such killing is not cruel. A person acts unnecessarily if the act is not required to terminate an animal's suffering, to protect the life or property of the actor or another person or if other means of disposing of an animal exist which would not impair the health or well-being of that animal.

Paragraphs (1), (2) and (4) of this subsection are inapplicable to accepted veterinary practices and activities carried on for scientific research.

Cruelty to animals is a class A misdemeanor, unless the person intentionally kills or causes serious injury to any animal in violation of paragraph (4) of this subsection, in which case it is a class F felony.

(c) Any person convicted of a misdemeanor violation of this section shall be prohibited from owning or possessing any animal for 5 years after said conviction, except for animals grown, raised or produced within the State for resale, or for sale of a product thereof, where the person has all necessary licenses for such sale or resale, and receives at least 25 percent of the person's annual gross income from such sale or resale.

A violation of this subsection is subject to a fine in the amount of $1,000 in any court of competent jurisdiction and to forfeiture of any animal illegally owned in accordance with the provisions of 3 Del. C. s 7907.

(d) Any person convicted of a felony violation of this section shall be prohibited from owning or possessing any animal for 15 years after said conviction, except for animals grown, raised or produced within the State for resale, or for sale of a product thereof, where the person has all necessary licenses for such sale or resale, and receives at least 25 percent of the person's annual gross income from such sale or resale.

A violation of this subsection is subject to a fine in the amount of $5,000 in any court of competent jurisdiction and to forfeiture of any animal illegally owned in accordance with the provisions of 3 Del. C. s 7907.

(e) Any agent of the Delaware Society for the Prevention of Cruelty to Animals, or, in Kent County of this State, of the Kent County Society for the Prevention of Cruelty to Animals, may impound an animal owned or possessed in apparent violation of this section, consistent with 3 Del. C. s 7907.

(f) This section shall not apply to the lawful hunting or trapping of animals as provided by law.

DISTRICT OF COLUMBIA CODE 1981 § 22-801 DEFINITION AND PENALTY.

Whoever overdrives, overloads, drives when overloaded, overworks, tortures, torments, deprives of necessary sustenance, cruelly beats, mutilates, or cruelly kills, or causes or procures to be so overdriven, overloaded, driven when overloaded, overworked, tortured, tormented, deprived of necessary sustenance, cruelly beaten, mutilated, or cruelly killed any animal, and whoever, having the charge or custody of any animal, either as owner or otherwise, inflicts unnecessary cruelty upon the same, or unnecessarily fails to provide the same with proper food, drink, shelter, or protection from the weather, shall for every such offense be punished by imprisonment in jail not exceeding 180 days, or by fine not exceeding $250, or by both such fine and imprisonment.

FLORIDA STATUTES§ 828.12. CRUELTY TO ANIMALS.

(1) A person who unnecessarily overloads, overdrives, torments, deprives of necessary sustenance or shelter, or unnecessarily mutilates, or kills any animal, or causes the same to be done, or carries in or upon any vehicle, or otherwise, any animal in a cruel or inhumane manner, is guilty of a misdemeanor of the first degree, punishable as provided in s. 775.082 or by a fine of not more than $5,000, or both.

(2) A person who intentionally commits an act to any animal which results in the cruel death, or excessive or repeated infliction of unnecessary pain or suffering, or causes the same to be done, is guilty of a

felony of the third degree, punishable as provided in s. 775.082 or by a fine of not more than $10,000, or both.

(3) A veterinarian licensed to practice in the state shall be held harmless from either criminal or civil liability for any decisions made or services rendered under the provisions of this section. Such a veterinarian is, therefore, under this subsection, immune from a lawsuit for his part in an investigation of cruelty to animals.

CODE OF GEORGIA § 16-12-4 CRUELTY TO ANIMALS.

(a) A person is guilty of a misdemeanor of cruelty to animals in the second degree when his act, omission, or neglect causes unjustifiable physical pain, suffering, or death to any living animal.

(b) A person is guilty of a misdemeanor of cruelty to animals in the first degree upon a second or subsequent violation of subsection (a) of this Code section and, upon conviction, may be punished by imprisonment not to exceed 12 months or a fine not to exceed $5,000.00 or both.

(c) This Code section does not apply to the killing of animals raised for the purpose of providing food nor does it apply to any person who hunts wild animals in compliance with the game and fish laws of this state. The killing or injuring of an animal for humane purposes or in the furtherance of medical or scientific research is justifiable.

HAWAII REVISED STATUTES § 711-1109 CRUELTY TO ANIMALS.

(1) A person commits the offense of cruelty to animals if the person intentionally, knowingly or recklessly:

(a) Overdrives, overloads, tortures, torments, cruelly beats or starves any animal or causes or procures the overdriving, overloading, torture, torment, cruel beating or starving of any animal;

(b) Mutilates, poisons, or kills without need any animal other than insects, vermin, or other pests;

(c) Keeps, uses or in any way is connected with or interested in the management of, or receives money for the admission of any person to, any place kept or used for the purpose of fighting or baiting any bull, bear, dog, cock or other animal, and every person who encourages, aids or assists therein, or who permits or suffers any place to be so kept or used;

(d) Carries or causes to be carried, in or upon any vehicle or other conveyance, any animal in a cruel or inhumane manner; or

(e) Assists another in the commission of any act of cruelty to any animal.

(2) Subsection (1)(a), (b), (d), (e) and the following subsection (3) are not applicable to accepted veterinary practices and to activities carried on for scientific research governed by standards of accepted educational or medicinal practices.

(3) Whenever any domestic animal is so severely injured that there is no reasonable probability that its life or usefulness can be saved, the animal may be immediately destroyed.

(4) Cruelty to animals is a misdemeanor.

IDAHO CODE § 25-3504 COMMITTING CRUELTY TO ANIMALS.

Every person who is cruel to any animal, or causes or procures any animal to be cruelly treated; and whoever, having the charge or custody of any animal, either as owner or otherwise, subjects any animal to cruelty, is, for every such offense, guilty of a misdemeanor and shall, upon conviction, be punished in accordance with section 25-3520A, Idaho Code.

ILLINOIS COMPILED STATUTES § 70/3.02. AGGRAVATED CRUELTY.

No person may intentionally commit an act that causes a companion animal to suffer serious injury or death. Aggravated cruelty does not include euthanasia of a companion animal through recognized methods approved by the Department of Agriculture.

INDIANA CODE § 35-46-3-12 TORTURE, MUTILATION OR KILLING OF VERTEBRATE ANIMAL.

(a) A person who knowingly or intentionally:

(1) tortures, beats, or mutilates a vertebrate animal resulting in serious injury or death to the animal; or

(2) kills a vertebrate animal without the authority of the owner of the animal; commits cruelty to an animal, a Class A misdemeanor.

(b) It is a defense that the accused person reasonably believes the conduct was necessary to:

(1) prevent injury to the accused person or another person;

(2) protect the property of the accused person from destruction or substantial damage; or

(3) prevent a seriously injured vertebrate animal from prolonged suffering.

IOWA CODE § 717.2. LIVESTOCK NEGLECT.

1. A person who impounds or confines livestock, in any place, and does any of the following commits the offense of livestock neglect:

a. Fails to provide livestock with care consistent with customary animal husbandry practices.

b. Deprives livestock of necessary sustenance.

c. Injures or destroys livestock by any means which causes pain or suffering in a manner inconsistent with customary animal husbandry practices.

2. A person who commits the offense of livestock neglect is guilty of a simple misdemeanor. A person who intentionally commits the offense of livestock neglect which results in serious injury to or the death of livestock is guilty of a serious misdemeanor. However, a person shall not be guilty of more than one offense of livestock neglect punishable as a serious misdemeanor, when care or sustenance is not provided to multiple head of livestock during any period of uninterrupted neglect.

3. This section does not apply to an institution, as defined in section 145B.1, or a research facility, as defined in section 162.2, provided that the institution or research facility performs functions within the scope of accepted practices and disciplines associated with the institution or research facility.

KANSAS STATUTES § 21-4310. CRUELTY TO ANIMALS.

(a) Cruelty to animals is:

(1) Intentionally killing, injuring, maiming, torturing or mutilating any animal;

(2) abandoning or leaving any animal in any place without making provisions for its proper care; or

(3) having physical custody of any animal and failing to provide such food, potable water, protection from the elements, opportunity for exercise and other care as is needed for the health or well-being of such kind of animal.

(b) The provisions of this section shall not apply to:

(1) Normal or accepted veterinary practices;

(2) bona fide experiments carried on by commonly recognized research facilities;

(3) killing, attempting to kill, trapping, catching or taking of any animal in accordance with the provisions of chapter 32 or chapter 47 of the Kansas Statutes Annotated;

(4) rodeo practices accepted by the rodeo cowboys' association;

(5) the humane killing of an animal which is diseased or disabled beyond recovery for any useful purpose, or the humane killing of animals for population control, by the owner thereof or the agent of such owner residing outside of a city or the owner thereof within a city if no animal shelter, pound or licensed veterinarian is within the city, or by a licensed veterinarian at the request of the owner thereof, or by any officer or agent of an incorporated humane society, the operator of an animal shelter or pound, a local or state health officer or a licensed veterinarian three business days following the receipt of any such animal at such society, shelter or pound;

(6) with respect to farm animals, normal or accepted practices of animal husbandry;

(7) the killing of any animal by any person at any time which may be found outside of the owned or rented property of the owner or custodian of such animal and which is found injuring or posing a threat to any person, farm animal or property; or

(8) an animal control officer trained by a licensed veterinarian in the use of a tranquilizer gun, using such gun with the appropriate dosage for the size of the animal, when such animal is vicious or could not be captured after reasonable attempts using other methods.

(c) Cruelty to animals is a class A nonperson misdemeanor.

KENTUCKY REVISED STATUTES § 525.125. CRUELTY TO ANIMALS IN THE FIRST DEGREE.

(1) The following persons are guilty of cruelty to animals in the first degree whenever a four-legged animal is caused to fight for pleasure or profit:

(a) The owner of the animal;

(b) The owner of the property on which the fight is conducted if the owner knows of the fight;

(c) Anyone who participates in the organization of the fight.

(2) Activities of animals engaged in hunting, field trials, dog training, and other activities authorized either by a hunting license or by the Department of Fish and Wildlife shall not constitute a violation of this section.

(3) Cruelty to animals in the first degree is a Class D felony.

§ 525.130. Cruelty to animals in the second degree.

(1) A person is guilty of cruelty to animals in the second degree when except as authorized by law he intentionally or wantonly:

(a) Subjects any animal to or causes cruel or injurious mistreatment through abandonment, participates other than as provided in KRS 525.125 in causing it to fight for pleasure or profit, (including, but not limited to being a spectator or vendor at an event where a four (4) legged animal is caused to fight for pleasure or profit) mutilation, beating, torturing, tormenting, failing to provide adequate food, drink, space, or health care, or by any other means; or

(b) Subjects any animal in his custody to cruel neglect; or

(c) Kills any animal.

(2) Nothing in this section shall apply to the killing of animals:

(a) Pursuant to a license to hunt, fish, or trap;

(b) Incident to the processing as food or for other commercial purposes;

(c) For humane purposes;

(d) For any other purpose authorized by law.

(3) Activities of animals engaged in hunting, field trials, dog training, and other activities authorized either by a hunting license or by the Department of Fish and Wildlife shall not constitute a violation of this section.

(4) Cruelty to animals in the second degree is a Class A misdemeanor.

LOUISIANA REVISED STATUTES § 102.1. CRUELTY TO ANIMALS; SIMPLE AND AGGRAVATED.

A. (1) Any person who intentionally or with criminal negligence commits any of the following shall be guilty of simple cruelty to animals:

(a) Overdrives, overloads, drives when overloaded, or overworks a living animal.

(b) Torments, cruelly beats, or unjustifiably injures any living animal, whether belonging to himself or another.

(c) Having charge, custody, or possession of any animal, either as owner or otherwise, unjustifiably fails to provide it with proper food, proper drink, [FN1] proper shelter, or proper veterinary care.

(d) Abandons any animal. A person shall not be considered to have abandoned an animal if he delivers to an animal control center an animal which he found running at large.

(e) Impounds or confines or causes to be impounded or confined in a pound or other place, a living animal and fails to supply it during such confinement with proper food, proper drink, [FN1] and proper shelter.

(f) Carries, or causes to be carried, a living animal in or upon a vehicle or otherwise, in a cruel or inhumane manner.

(g) Unjustifiably administers any poisonous or noxious drug or substance to any domestic animal or unjustifiably exposes any such drug or substance, with intent that the same shall be taken or swallowed by any domestic animal.

(h) Injures any animal belonging to another person without legal privilege or consent of the owner.

(i) Mistreats any living animal by any act or omission whereby unnecessary or unjustifiable physical pain, suffering, or death is caused to or permitted upon the animal.

(j) Causes or procures to be done by any person any act enumerated in this Subsection.

A. (2)(a) Whoever commits the crime of simple cruelty to animals shall be fined not more than one thousand dollars, or imprisoned for not more than six months, or both.

(b) In addition to any other penalty imposed, a person who commits the crime of cruelty to animals shall be ordered to perform five eight-hour days of court-approved community service. The community service requirement shall not be suspended.

B. (1) Any person who intentionally or with criminal negligence tortures, maims, mutilates, or maliciously kills any living animal, whether belonging to himself or another, shall be guilty of aggravated cruelty to animals.

B. (2) Any person who causes or procures to be done by any person any act designated in this Subsection shall also be guilty of aggravated cruelty to animals.

B. (3) Whoever commits the crime of aggravated cruelty to animals shall be fined not less than one thousand dollars nor more than twenty-five thousand dollars or imprisoned, with or without hard labor, for not less than one year nor more than ten years, or both.

B. (4) For purposes of this Subsection, where more than one animal is tortured, maimed, mutilated, or maliciously killed, each act comprises a separate offense.

C. This Section shall not apply to the lawful hunting or trapping of wildlife as provided by law, herding of domestic animals, accepted veterinary practices, and activities carried on for scientific or medical research governed by accepted standards.

D. For purposes of this Section, fowl shall not be defined as animals. Only the following birds shall be identified as animals for purposes of this Section:

(1) Order Psittaciformes-parrots, parakeets, lovebirds, macaws, cockatiels or cockatoos.

(2) Order Passeriformes-canaries, starlings, sparrows, flycatchers, mynah or myna.

MAINE REVISED STATUTES § 4011. CRUELTY TO ANIMALS.

1. Cruelty to animals. Except as provided in subsection 1-A, a person, including an owner or the owner's agent, is guilty of cruelty to animals if that person:

A. Kills or attempts to kill any animal belonging to another person without the consent of the owner or without legal privilege;

B. Except for a licensed veterinarian or a person certified under Title 17, section 1042, kills or attempts to kill an animal by a method that does not cause instantaneous death;

C. If that person is a licensed veterinarian or a person certified under Title 17, section 1042, kills or attempts to kill an animal by a method that causes undue suffering. The commissioner shall adopt rules that define "undue suffering";

D. Injures, overworks, tortures, torments, abandons or cruelly beats or mutilates an animal; gives drugs to an animal with an intent to harm the animal; gives poison or alcohol to an animal; or exposes a poison with intent that it be taken by an animal. The owner or occupant of property is privileged to use reasonable force to eject a trespassing animal;

E. Deprives an animal that the person owns or possesses of necessary sustenance, necessary medical attention, proper shelter, protection from the weather or humanely clean conditions; or

F. Keeps or leaves a domestic animal on an uninhabited or barren island lying off the coast of the State during the month of December,

January, February or March without providing necessary sustenance and proper shelter.

1-A. Animal cruelty. Except as provided in paragraphs A and B, a person is guilty of cruelty to animals if that person kills or attempts to kill a cat or dog.

A. A licensed veterinarian or a person certified under Title 17, section 1042 may kill a cat or dog according to the methods of euthanasia under Title 17, chapter 42, subchapter IV. [FN1]

B. A person who owns a cat or dog, or the owner's agent, may kill that owner's cat or dog by shooting with a firearm provided the following conditions are met.

(1) The shooting is performed by a person 18 years of age or older using a weapon and ammunition of suitable caliber and other characteristics to produce instantaneous death by a single shot.

(2) Death is instantaneous.

(3) Maximum precaution is taken to protect the general public, employees and other animals.

(4) Any restraint of the cat or dog during the shooting does not cause undue suffering to the cat or dog.

2. Affirmative defenses. It is an affirmative defense to this section that:

A. The conduct was performed by a licensed veterinarian or was a part of scientific research governed by accepted standards;

B. The conduct was designed to control or eliminate rodents, ants or other common pests on the defendant's own property; or

C. The conduct involved the use of live animals as bait or in the training of other animals in accordance with the laws of the Department of Inland Fisheries and Wildlife, Title 12, Part 10. [FN1]

Evidence of proper care of any animal shall not be admissible in the defense of alleged cruelty to other animals.

TITLE 17. CRIMES § 1031. Cruelty to animals.

1. Cruelty to animals. Except as provided in subsection 1-A, a person, including an owner or the owner's agent, is guilty of cruelty to animals if that person:

A. Kills or attempts to kill any animal belonging to another person without the consent of the owner or without legal privilege;

B. Except for a licensed veterinarian or a person certified under section 1042, kills or attempts to kill an animal by a method that does not cause instantaneous death;

C. If that person is a licensed veterinarian or a person certified under section 1042, kills or attempts to kill an animal by a method that causes undue suffering. The commissioner shall adopt rules that define "undue suffering";

D. Injures, overworks, tortures, torments, abandons or cruelly beats or mutilates an animal; gives drugs to an animal with an intent to harm the animal; gives poison or alcohol to an animal; or exposes a poison with intent that it be taken by an animal. The owner or occupant of property is privileged to use reasonable force to eject a trespassing animal;

E. Deprives an animal that the person owns or possesses of necessary sustenance, necessary medical attention, proper shelter, protection from the weather or humanely clean conditions; or

F. Keeps or leaves a domestic animal on an uninhabited or barren island lying off the coast of the State during the month of December, January, February or March without providing necessary sustenance and proper shelter.

1-A. Animal cruelty. Except as provided in paragraphs A and B, a person is guilty of cruelty to animals if that person kills or attempts to kill a cat or dog.

A. A licensed veterinarian or a person certified under section 1042 may kill a cat or dog according to the methods of euthanasia under chapter 42, subchapter IV. [FN1]

B. A person who owns a cat or dog, or the owner's agent, may kill that owner's cat or dog by shooting with a firearm provided the following conditions are met.

(1) The shooting is performed by a person 18 years of age or older using a weapon and ammunition of suitable caliber and other characteristics to produce instantaneous death by a single shot.

(2) Death is instantaneous.

(3) Maximum precaution is taken to protect the general public, employees and other animals.

(4) Any restraint of the cat or dog during the shooting does not cause undue suffering.

2. Affirmative defense. It is an affirmative defense to prosecution under this section that:

A. The defendant's conduct conformed to accepted veterinary practice or was a part of scientific research governed by accepted standards;

B. The defendant's conduct or that of his agent was designed to control or eliminate rodents, ants or other common pests on his own property; or

C. The defendant's conduct involved the use of live animals as bait or in the training of other animals in accordance with the laws of the Department of Inland Fisheries and Wildlife, Title 12, Part 10. [FN2]

Evidence of proper care of any animal shall not be admissible in the defense of alleged cruelty to other animals.

3. Penalty. Cruelty to animals is a Class D crime. In addition to any other penalty authorized by law, the court shall impose a fine of not less than $100 for each violation of this section.

4. Criminal or civil prosecution. A person may be arrested or detained for the crime of cruelty to animals in accordance with the rules of criminal procedure. No person may be arrested or detained for the civil violation of cruelty to animals. The attorney for the State shall elect to charge a defendant with the crime of cruelty to animals under this section or the civil violation of cruelty to animals under Title 7, section 4011. In making this election, the attorney for the State shall consider the severity of the cruelty displayed, the number of animals involved, any prior convictions or adjudications of animal cruelty entered against the defendant and such other factors as may be relevant to a determination of whether criminal or civil sanctions will best accomplish the goals of the animal welfare laws in the particular case before the attorney for the State. The election and determination required by this subsection shall not be subject to judicial review. The factors involved in such election and determination are not elements of the criminal offense or civil violation of animal cruelty and are not subject to proof or disproof as prerequisites or conditions for conviction under this subsection or adjudication under Title 7, section 4011.

CODE OF MARYLAND § 59 CRUELTY TO ANIMALS A MISDEMEANOR.

(a) Cruelty. — Any person who

(1) overdrives, overloads, deprives of necessary sustenance, tortures, torments, or cruelly beats; or

(2) causes, procures or authorizes these acts; or

(3) having the charge or custody of an animal, either as owner or otherwise, inflicts unnecessary suffering or pain upon the animal, or unnecessarily fails to provide the animal with nutritious food in sufficient quantity, necessary veterinary care, proper drink, air, space, shelter or protection from the weather; or

(4) uses or permits to be used any bird, fowl, or cock for the purpose of fighting with any other animal, which is commonly known as cockfighting, is guilty of a misdemeanor punishable by a fine not exceeding $1,000 or by imprisonment not to exceed 90 days, or both.

(b) Mutilation. —Any person who

(1) intentionally mutilates or cruelly kills an animal, or causes, procures, or authorizes the cruel killing or intentional mutilation of an animal; or

(2) uses or permits a dog to be used in or arranges or conducts a dogfight, is guilty of a misdemeanor punishable by a fine not exceeding $5,000 or by imprisonment not to exceed 3 years, or both.

(c) Customary and normal veterinary and agricultural husbandry practices.—Customary and normal veterinary and agricultural husbandry practices including but not limited to dehorning, castration, docking tails, and limit feeding, are not covered by the provisions of this section. In the case of activities in which physical pain may unavoidably be caused to animals, such as food processing, pest elimination, animal training, and hunting, cruelty shall mean a failure to employ the most humane method reasonably available. It is the intention of the General Assembly that all animals, whether they be privately owned, strays, domesticated, feral, farm, corporately or institutionally owned, under private, local, State, or federally funded scientific or medical activities, or otherwise being situated in Maryland shall be protected from intentional cruelty, but that no person shall be liable for criminal prosecution for normal human activities to which the infliction of pain to an animal is purely incidental and unavoidable.

MASSACHUSETTS GENERAL LAWS § 77. CRUELTY TO ANIMALS.

Whoever overdrives, overloads, drives when overloaded, overworks, tortures, torments, deprives of necessary sustenance, cruelly beats, mutilates or kills an animal, or causes or procures an animal to be overdriven, overloaded, driven when overloaded, overworked, tortured, tormented, deprived of necessary sustenance, cruelly beaten, mutilated or killed; and whoever uses in a cruel or inhuman manner in a race, game, or contest, or in training therefor, as lure or bait a live animal, except an animal if used as lure or bait in fishing; and whoever, having the charge or custody of an animal, either as owner or otherwise, inflicts unnecessary cruelty upon it, or unnecessarily fails to provide it with proper food, drink, shelter, sanitary environment, or protection from the weather, and whoever, as owner, possessor, or person having the charge or custody of an animal, cruelly drives or works it when unfit for labor, or willfully abandons it, or carries it or causes it to be carried in or upon a vehicle, or otherwise, in an unnecessarily cruel or inhuman manner or in a way and manner which might endanger the animal carried thereon, or knowingly and willfully authorizes or permits it to be subjected to unnecessary torture, suffering or cruelty of any kind shall be punished by a fine of not more than one thousand dollars or by imprisonment for not more than one year, or both.

In addition to any other penalty provided by law, upon conviction for any violation of this section or of sections seventy-seven A, seventy-eight, seventy-eight A, seventy-nine A, seventy-nine B, eighty A, eighty B, eighty C, eighty D, eighty F, eighty-six, eighty-six A, eighty-six B or ninety-four the defendant may, after an appropriate hearing to determine the defendant's fitness for continued custody of the abused animal, be ordered to surrender or forfeit to the custody of any society, incorporated under the laws of the commonwealth for the prevention of cruelty to animals or for the care and protection of homeless or suffering animals, the animal whose treatment was the basis of such conviction.

MICHIGAN COMPILED LAWS § 750.50. DEFINITIONS; CRIMES AGAINST ANIMALS, CRUEL TREATMENT, ABANDONMENT, FAILURE TO PROVIDE ADEQUATE CARE; PENALTIES, MISDEMEANOR, PAYMENT OF COSTS; EXCEPTIONS.

(1) As used in this section and section 50b:

(a) "Adequate care" means the provision of sufficient food, water, shelter, sanitary conditions, and veterinary medical attention in order to maintain an animal in a state of good health.

(b) "Animal" means any vertebrate other than a human being.

(c) "Livestock" has the meaning attributed to the term in the animal industry act of 1987, Act No. 466 of the Public Acts of 1988, being sections 287.701 to 287.747 of the Michigan Compiled Laws.

(d) "Person" means an individual, partnership, limited liability company, corporation, association, governmental entity, or other legal entity.

(e) "Neglect" means to fail to sufficiently and properly care for an animal to the extent that the animal's health is jeopardized.

(f) "Sanitary conditions" means space free from health hazards including excessive animal waste, overcrowding of animals, or other conditions that endanger the animal's health. This definition does not include a condition resulting from a customary and reasonable practice pursuant to farming or animal husbandry.

(g) "Shelter" means adequate protection from the elements suitable for the age and species of animal and weather conditions to maintain the animal in a state of good health, including structures or natural features such as trees and topography.

(h) "State of good health" means freedom from disease and illness, and in a condition of proper body weight and temperature for the age and species of the animal, unless the animal is undergoing appropriate treatment.

(i) "Water" means potable water that is suitable for the age and species of animal, made regularly available unless otherwise directed by a veterinarian licensed to practice veterinary medicine.

(2) An owner, possessor, or person having the charge or custody of an animal shall not do any of the following:

(a) Fail to provide an animal with adequate care.

(b) Cruelly drive, work, or beat an animal, or cause an animal to be cruelly driven, worked, or beaten.

(c) Carry or cause to be carried in or upon a vehicle or otherwise any live animal having the feet or legs tied together, other than an animal being transported for medical care, or a horse whose feet are hobbled to protect the horse during transport or in any other cruel and inhumane manner.

(d) Carry or cause to be carried a live animal in or upon a vehicle or otherwise without providing a secure space, rack, car, crate, or cage, in which livestock may stand, and in which all other animals may stand, turn around, and lie down during transportation, or while awaiting slaughter. As used in this subdivision, for purposes of transportation of sled dogs, "stand" means sufficient vertical distance to allow the animal to stand without its shoulders touching the top of the crate or transportation vehicle.

(e) Abandon an animal or cause an animal to be abandoned, in any place, without making provisions for the animal's adequate care, unless premises are temporarily vacated for the protection of human life during a disaster. An animal that is lost by an owner or custodian while traveling, walking, hiking or hunting shall not be regarded as abandoned under this section when the owner or custodian has made a reasonable effort to locate the animal.

(f) Willfully or negligently allow any animal, including one who is aged, diseased, maimed, hopelessly sick, disabled, or nonambulatory to suffer unnecessary neglect, torture, or pain .

(3) A person who violates subsection (2) is guilty of a misdemeanor, punishable by imprisonment for not more than 93 days, or by a fine of not more than $1,000.00, or community service not to exceed 200 hours, or any combination of these penalties.

(4) As a part of the sentence for a violation of subsection (2), the court may order the defendant to pay the costs of the prosecution and the costs of the care, housing, and veterinary medical care for the animal, as applicable. If the court does not order a defendant to pay all of the applicable costs listed in this subsection, or orders only partial payment of these costs, the court shall state on the record the reason for that action.

(5) As a part of the sentence for a violation of subsection (2), the court may, as a condition of probation, order the defendant not to own or possess an animal for a period of time not to exceed the period of probation.

(6) A person who owns or possesses an animal in violation of an order issued under subsection (5) is subject to revocation of probation.

(7) This section does not prohibit the lawful use of an animal, including, but not limited to, the following:

(a) Fishing.

(b) Hunting, trapping, or wildlife control.

(c) Horse racing.

(d) The operation of a zoological park or aquarium.

(e) Pest or rodent control.

(f) Scientific research.

(g) Farming or animal husbandry.

MINNESOTA STATUTES § 343.21. OVERWORKING OR MISTREATING ANIMALS; PENALTY.

Subdivision 1. Torture. No person shall overdrive, overload, torture, cruelly beat, neglect, or unjustifiably injure, maim, mutilate, or kill any animal, or cruelly work any animal when it is unfit for labor, whether it belongs to that person or to another person.

Subdivision 2. Nourishment; shelter. No person shall deprive any animal over which the person has charge or control of necessary food, water, or shelter.

Subdivision 3. Enclosure. No person shall keep any cow or other animal in any enclosure without providing wholesome exercise and change of air.

Subdivision 4. Low feed. No person shall feed any cow on food which produces impure or unwholesome milk.

Subdivision 5. Abandonment. No person shall abandon any animal.

Subdivision 6. Temporary abandonment. No person shall allow any maimed, sick, infirm, or disabled animal to lie in any street, road, or other public place for more than three hours after receiving notice of the animal's condition.

Subdivision 7. Cruelty. No person shall willfully instigate or in any way further any act of cruelty to any animal or animals, or any act tending to produce cruelty to animals.

Subdivision 8. Caging. No person shall cage any animal for public display purposes unless the display cage is constructed of solid material on three sides to protect the caged animal from the elements and unless the horizontal dimension of each side of the cage is at least four times the length of the caged animal. The provisions of this subdivision do not apply to the Minnesota state agricultural society, the Minnesota state fair, or to the county agricultural societies, county fairs, to any agricultural display of caged animals by any political subdivision of the state of Minnesota, or to district, regional or national educational livestock or poultry exhibitions. The provisions of this subdivision do not apply to captive wildlife, the exhibition of which is regulated by section 97A.041.

Subdivision 9. Penalty. A person who fails to comply with any provision of this section is guilty of a misdemeanor. A person convicted of a second or subsequent violation of subdivision 1 or 7 within five years of a previous violation of subdivision 1 or 7 is guilty of a gross misdemeanor.

Subdivision 10. Restrictions. If a person is convicted of violating this section, the court shall require that pet or companion animals, as defined in section 346.36, subdivision 6, that have not been seized by a peace officer or agent and are in the custody of the person must be turned over to a peace officer or other appropriate officer or agent unless the court determines that the person is able and fit to provide adequately for an animal. If the evidence indicates lack of proper and reasonable care of an animal, the burden is on the person to affirmatively demonstrate by clear and convincing evidence that the person is able and fit to have custody of and provide adequately for an animal. The court may limit the person's further possession or custody of pet or companion animals, and may impose other conditions the court considers appropriate, including, but not limited to:

(1) imposing a probation period during which the person may not have ownership, custody, or control of a pet or companion animal;

(2) requiring periodic visits of the person by an animal control officer or agent appointed pursuant to section 343.01, subdivision 1;

(3) requiring performance by the person of community service in a humane facility; and

(4) requiring the person to receive behavioral counseling.

MISSISSIPPI CODE 1972 § 97-41-1. LIVING CREATURES NOT TO BE CRUELLY TREATED.

If any person shall override, overdrive, overload, torture, torment, unjustifiably injure, deprive of necessary sustenance, food, or drink; or cruelly beat or needlessly mutilate; or cause or procure to be overridden, overdriven, overloaded, tortured, unjustifiably injured, tormented, or deprived of necessary sustenance, food or drink; or to be cruelly beaten or needlessly mutilated or killed, any living creature, every such offender shall, for every offense, be guilty of a misdemeanor.

MISSOURI STATUTES § 578.009. ANIMAL NEGLECT—PENALTIES.

1. A person is guilty of animal neglect when he has custody or ownership or both of an animal and fails to provide adequate care or adequate control, including, but not limited to, knowingly abandoning an animal in any place without making provisions for its adequate care which results in substantial harm to the animal.

2. Animal neglect is a class C misdemeanor upon first conviction and for each offense, punishable by imprisonment or a fine not to exceed five hundred dollars, or both, and a class B misdemeanor punishable by imprisonment or a fine not to exceed one thousand dollars, or both upon the second and all subsequent convictions. All fines and penalties for a first conviction of animal neglect may be waived by the court provided that the person found guilty of animal neglect shows that adequate, permanent remedies for the neglect have been made. Reasonable costs incurred for the care and maintenance of neglected animals may not be waived.

§ 578.012. Animal abuse—penalties.

1. A person is guilty of animal abuse when a person:

(1) Intentionally or purposely kills an animal in any manner not allowed by or expressly exempted from the provisions of sections 578.005 to 578.023 and 273.030, RSMo:

(2) Purposely or intentionally causes injury or suffering to an animal; or

(3) Having ownership or custody of an animal knowingly fails to provide adequate care or adequate control.

2. Animal abuse is a class A misdemeanor, unless the defendant has previously plead guilty to or has been found guilty of animal abuse or the suffering involved in subdivision (2) of subsection 1 of this section is the result of torture and mutilation consciously inflicted while the animal was alive, in which case it is a class D felony.

3. For purposes of this section, "animal" shall be defined as a mammal.

MONTANA CODE § 45-8-211. CRUELTY TO ANIMALS—EXCEPTION.

(1) A person commits the offense of cruelty to animals if without justification the person knowingly or negligently subjects an animal to mistreatment or neglect by:

(a) overworking, beating, tormenting, injuring, or killing any animal;

(b) carrying or confining any animal in a cruel manner;

(c) failing to provide an animal in the person's custody with:

(i) proper food, drink, or shelter; or

(ii) in cases of immediate, obvious, serious illness or injury, licensed veterinary or other appropriate medical care;

(d) abandoning any helpless animal or abandoning any animal on any highway, railroad, or in any other place where it may suffer injury, hunger, or exposure or become a public charge; or

(e) promoting, sponsoring, conducting, or participating in an animal race of more than 2 miles, except a sanctioned endurance race.

(2) (a) A person convicted of the offense of cruelty to animals shall be fined not to exceed $500 or be imprisoned in the county jail for a term not to exceed 6 months, or both. A person convicted of a second or subsequent offense of cruelty to animals shall be fined not to exceed $1,000 or be imprisoned in the state prison for a term not to exceed 2 years, or both.

(b) If the convicted person is the owner, the person may be required to forfeit to the county in which the person is convicted any animal affected. This provision does not affect the interest of any secured party or other person who has not participated in the offense.

(3) In addition to the sentence provided in subsection (2), the court may:

(a) require the defendant to pay all reasonable costs incurred in providing necessary veterinary attention and treatment for any animal affected; and

(b) prohibit or limit the defendant's ownership, possession, or custody of animals, as the court believes appropriate during the term of the sentence.

(4) Nothing in this section prohibits:

(a) a person from humanely destroying an animal for just cause; or

(b) the use of commonly accepted agricultural and livestock practices on livestock.

NEBRASKA REVISED STATUTES OF 1943 § 28-1009. CRUELTY TO ANIMALS; HARASSMENT OF A POLICE ANIMAL; PENALTY.

(1) A person commits cruelty to animals if he or she abandons, cruelly mistreats, or cruelly neglects an animal. Cruelty to animals is a Class II misdemeanor for the first offense and a Class I misdemeanor for any subsequent offense.

(2) A person commits harassment of a police animal if he or she knowingly and intentionally teases or harasses a police animal in order to distract, agitate, or harm the police animal for the purpose of preventing such animal from performing its legitimate official duties. Harassment of a police animal is a Class IV misdemeanor unless the harassment is the proximate cause of the death of the police animal, in which case it is a Class IV felony.

NEW HAMPSHIRE STATUTES§ 644:8. CRUELTY TO ANIMALS.

I. In this section, "cruelty" shall include, but not be limited to, acts or omissions injurious or detrimental to the health, safety or welfare of any animal, including the abandoning of any animal without proper provision for its care, sustenance, protection or shelter.

II. In this section, "animal" means a domestic animal, a household pet or a wild animal in captivity.

III. A person is guilty of a misdemeanor for a first offense, and of a class B felony for a second or subsequent offense, who:

(a) Without lawful authority negligently deprives or causes to be deprived any animal in his possession or custody necessary care, sustenance or shelter;

(b) Negligently beats, cruelly whips, tortures, mutilates or in any other manner mistreats or causes to be mistreated any animal;

(c) Negligently overdrives, overworks, drives when overloaded, or otherwise abuses or misuses any animal intended for or used for labor;

(d) Negligently transports any animal in his possession or custody in a manner injurious to the health, safety or physical well-being of such animal;

(e) Negligently abandons any animal previously in his possession or custody by causing such animal to be left without supervision or adequate provision for its care, sustenance or shelter; or

(f) Otherwise negligently permits or causes any animal in his possession or custody to be subjected to cruelty, inhumane treatment or unnecessary suffering of any kind.

III-a. A person is guilty of a class B felony who purposely beats, cruelly whips, tortures, or mutilates any animal or causes any animal to be beaten, cruelly whipped, tortured, or mutilated.

IV. In addition to being guilty of crimes as provided in paragraphs III and III-a, any person charged with cruelty to animals may have his animal confiscated by the arresting officer and, upon said person's conviction of cruelty to animals, the court may dispose of said animal in any manner it decides. The costs, if any, incurred in boarding and treating the animal, pending disposition of the case, and in disposing of the animal, upon a conviction of said person for cruelty to animals, shall be borne by the person so convicted.

IV-a. (a) Except as provided in subparagraph (b) any appropriate law enforcement officer, animal control officer, or officer of a duly licensed humane society may take into temporary protective custody any animal when there is probable cause to believe that it has been abused or neglected in violation of paragraphs III or III-a when there is a clear and imminent danger to the animal's health or life and there is not sufficient time to obtain a court order. Such officer shall leave a written notice indicating the type and number of animals taken into protective custody, the name of the officer, the time and date taken, the reason it was taken, the procedure to have the animal returned and any other relevant information. Such notice shall be left at the location where the animal was taken into custody. The officer shall provide for proper care and housing of any animal taken into protective custody under this paragraph. If, after 7 days, the animal has not been returned or claimed, the officer shall petition the municipal or district court seeking either permanent custody or a one-week extension of custody or shall file charges under this section. If a week's extension is granted by the court and after a period of 14 days the animal remains unclaimed, the title and custody of the animal shall rest with the officer on behalf of his department or society. The department or society may dispose of the animal in any lawful and humane manner as if it were the rightful owner. If after 14 days the officer or his department determines that charges should be filed under this section, he shall petition the court.

(b) For purposes of subparagraph (a) the appropriate law enforcement officer for domestic animals, as defined in RSA 436:1, II, or livestock, as defined in RSA 427:38, III, shall be a veterinarian licensed under RSA 332-B or the state veterinarian.

V. A veterinarian licensed to practice in the state shall be held harmless from either criminal or civil liability for any decisions made for services rendered under the provisions of this section or RSA 435:11-16. Such a veterinarian is, therefore, under this paragraph, protected from a lawsuit for his part in an investigation of cruelty to animals.

NEW JERSEY STATUTES § 4:22-17. CRUELTY IN GENERAL; DISORDERLY PERSONS OFFENSE.

A person who shall:

a. Overdrive, overload, drive when overloaded, overwork, torture, torment, deprive of necessary sustenance, unnecessarily or cruelly beat or otherwise abuse, or needlessly mutilate or kill, a living animal or creature;

b. Cause or procure any of such acts to be done; or

c. Inflict unnecessary cruelty upon a living animal or creature of which he has charge either as owner or otherwise, or unnecessarily fail to provide it with proper food, drink, shelter or protection from the weather—

Shall be guilty of a disorderly persons offense.

§ 4:22-18. Carrying animal in cruel manner; disorderly persons offense.

A person who shall carry, or cause to be carried, a living animal or creature in or upon a vehicle or otherwise, in a cruel or inhumane manner, shall be guilty of a disorderly persons offense.

§ 4:22-26. Acts constituting cruelty in general; penalty.

A person who shall:

a. Overdrive, overload, drive when overloaded, overwork, torture, torment, deprive of necessary sustenance, or cruelly beat or otherwise abuse or needlessly mutilate or kill a living animal or creature;

b. Cause or procure to be done by his agent, servant, employee or otherwise an act enumerated in subsection "a." of this section;

c. Inflict unnecessary cruelty upon a living animal or creature of which he has charge or custody either as owner or otherwise, or unnecessarily fail to provide it with proper food, drink, shelter or protection from the weather;

d. Receive or offer for sale a horse which by reason of disability, disease or lameness, or any other cause, could not be worked without violating the provisions of this article;

e. Keep, use, be connected with or interested in the management of, or receive money or other consideration for the admission of a person to, a place kept or used for the purpose of fighting or baiting a living animal or creature;

f. Be present and witness, pay admission to, encourage, aid or assist in an activity enumerated in subsection "e." of this section;

g. Permit or suffer a place owned or controlled by him to be used as provided in subsection "e." of this section;

h. Carry, or cause to be carried, a living animal or creature in or upon a vehicle or otherwise, in a cruel or inhuman manner;

i. Use a dog or dogs for the purpose of drawing or helping to draw a vehicle for business purposes;

j. Impound or confine or cause to be impounded or confined in a pound or other place a living animal or creature, and shall fail to supply it during such confinement with a sufficient quantity of good and wholesome food and water;

k. Abandon a maimed, sick, infirm or disabled animal or creature to die in a public place;

l. Willfully sell, or offer to sell, use, expose, or cause or permit to be sold or offered for sale, used or exposed, a horse or other animal having the disease known as glanders or farcy, or other contagious or infectious disease dangerous to the health or life of human beings or animals, or who shall, when any such disease is beyond recovery, refuse, upon demand, to deprive the animal of life;

m. Own, operate, manage or conduct a roadside stand or market for the sale of merchandise along a public street or highway; or a shopping mall, or a part of the premises thereof; and keep a living animal or creature confined, or allowed to roam in an area whether or not the area is enclosed, on these premises as an exhibit; except that this subsection shall not be applicable to: a pet shop licensed pursuant to P.L.1941, c. 151 (C. 4:19-15.1 et seq.); a person who keeps an animal, in a humane manner, for the purpose of the protection of the premises; or a recognized breeders' association, a 4-H club, an educational agricultural program, an equestrian team, a humane society or other similar charitable or nonprofit organization conducting an exhibition, show or performance;

n. Keep or exhibit a wild animal at a roadside stand or market located along a public street or highway of this State; a gasoline station; or a shopping mall, or a part of the premises thereof;

o. Sell, offer for sale, barter or give away or display live baby chicks, ducklings or other fowl or rabbits, turtles or chameleons which have been dyed or artificially colored or otherwise treated so as to impart to them an artificial color;

p. Use any animal, reptile, or fowl for the purpose of soliciting any alms, collections, contributions, subscriptions, donations, or payment of money except in connection with exhibitions, shows or performances conducted in a bona fide manner by recognized breeders' associations, 4-H clubs or other similar bona fide organizations;

q. Sell or offer for sale, barter, or give away living rabbits, turtles, baby chicks, ducklings or other fowl under two months of age, for use as household or domestic pets;

r. Sell, offer for sale, barter or give away living baby chicks, ducklings or other fowl, or rabbits, turtles or chameleons under two months of age for any purpose not prohibited by subsection q. of this section and who shall fail to provide proper facilities for the care of such animals;

s. Artificially mark sheep or cattle, or cause them to be marked, by cropping or cutting off both ears, cropping or cutting either ear more than one inch from the tip end thereof, or half cropping or cutting both ears or either ear more than one inch from the tip end thereof, or who shall have or keep in his possession sheep or cattle, which he claims to own, marked contrary to this subsection unless they were bought in market or of a stranger;

t. Abandon a domesticated animal;

u. For amusement or gain, cause, allow, or permit the fighting or baiting of a living animal or creature;

v. Own, possess, keep, train, promote, purchase, or knowingly sell a living animal or creature for the purpose of fighting or baiting that animal or creature; or

w. Gamble on the outcome of a fight involving a living animal or creature—

Shall forfeit and pay a sum not to exceed $250.00, except in the case of a violation of subsection "t." a mandatory sum of $500, and $1,000 if the violation occurs on or near a roadway, to be sued for and recovered, with costs, in a civil action by any person in the name of the New Jersey Society for the Prevention of Cruelty to Animals.

NEW MEXICO STATUTES 1978 § 30-18-1 CRUELTY TO ANIMALS.

Cruelty to animals consists of:

A. torturing, tormenting, depriving of necessary sustenance, cruelly beating, mutilating, cruelly killing or overdriving any animal;

B. unnecessarily failing to provide any animal with proper food or drink; or

C. cruelly driving or working any animal when such animal is unfit for labor.

Whoever commits cruelty to animals is guilty of a petty misdemeanor.

CONSOLIDATED LAWS OF NEW YORK § 353. OVERDRIVING, TORTURING AND INJURING ANIMALS; FAILURE TO PROVIDE PROPER SUSTENANCE.

A person who overdrives, overloads, tortures or cruelly beats or unjustifiably injures, maims, mutilates or kills any animal, whether wild or tame, and whether belonging to himself or to another, or deprives any animal of necessary sustenance, food or drink, or neglects or refuses to furnish it such sustenance or drink, or causes, procures or permits any animal to be overdriven, overloaded, tortured, cruelly beaten, or unjustifiably injured, maimed, mutilated or killed, or to be deprived of necessary food or drink, or who wilfully sets on foot, instigates, engages in, or in any way furthers any act of cruelty to any animal, or any act tending to produce such cruelty, is guilty of a misdemeanor, punishable by imprisonment for not more than one year, or by a fine of not more than one thousand dollars, or by both.

Nothing herein contained shall be construed to prohibit or interfere with any properly conducted scientific tests, experiments or investigations, involving the use of living animals, performed or conducted in laboratories or institutions, which are approved for these purposes by the state commissioner of health. The state commissioner of health shall prescribe the rules under which such approvals shall be granted, including therein standards regarding the care and treatment of any such animals. Such rules shall be published and copies thereof conspicuously posted in each such laboratory or institution. The state commissioner of health or his duly authorized representative shall have the power to inspect such laboratories or institutions to insure compliance with such rules and standards. Each such approval may be revoked at any time for failure to comply with such rules and in any case the approval shall be limited to a period not exceeding one year.

NEVADA REVISED STATUTES § 574.100. OVERDRIVING, TORTURING, INJURING OR ABANDONING ANIMALS; FAILURE TO PROVIDE PROPER SUSTENANCE; PENALTY.

Except in any case involving a willful or malicious act for which a greater penalty is provided by NRS 206.150, a person who:

1. Overdrives, overloads, tortures or cruelly beats or unjustifiably injures, maims, mutilates or kills any animal, whether belonging to himself or to another;

2. Deprives any animal of necessary sustenance, food or drink, or neglects or refuses to furnish it such sustenance or drink;

3. Causes, procures or permits any animal to be overdriven, overloaded, tortured, cruelly beaten, or unjustifiably injured, maimed, mutilated or killed, or to be deprived of necessary food or drink;

4. Willfully sets on foot, instigates, engages in, or in any way furthers an act of cruelty to any animal, or any act tending to produce such cruelty; or

5. Abandons an animal in circumstances other than those prohibited in NRS 574.110, is guilty of a misdemeanor.

GENERAL STATUTES OF NORTH CAROLINA § 14-360 Cruelty to animals; construction of section.

If any person shall willfully overdrive, overload, wound, injure, torture, torment, deprive of necessary sustenance, cruelly beat, needlessly mutilate or kill or cause or procure to be overdriven, overloaded, wounded, injured, tortured, tormented, deprived of necessary sustenance, cruelly beaten, needlessly mutilated or killed as aforesaid, any useful beast, fowl or animal, every such offender shall for every such offense be guilty of a Class 1 misdemeanor. In this section, and in every law which may be enacted relating to animals, the words "animal" and "dumb animal" shall be held to include every living creature; the words "torture," "torment" or "cruelty" shall be held to include every act, omission or neglect whereby unjustifiable physical pain, suffering or death is caused or permitted. Such terms shall not be construed to prohibit the lawful taking of animals under the jurisdiction and regulation of the Wildlife Resources Commission.

NORTH DAKOTA CENTURY CODE § 36-21.1-02 OVERWORKING OR MISTREATING ANIMALS.

1. No person may overdrive, overload, torture, cruelly beat, neglect, or unjustifiably injure, maim, mutilate, or kill any animal, or cruelly work any animal when unfit for labor.

2. No person may deprive any animal over which he has charge or control of necessary food, water, or shelter.

3. No person may keep any animal in any enclosure without exercise and wholesome change of air.

4. No person may abandon any animal.

5. No person may allow any maimed, sick, infirm, or disabled animal of which he is the owner, or of which he has custody, to lie in any street, road, or other public place for more than three hours after notice.

6. No person may willfully instigate, or in any way further, any act of cruelty to any animal or animals, or any act tending to produce such cruelty.

7. No person may cage any animal for public display purposes unless the display cage is constructed of solid material on three sides to protect the caged animal from the elements, and unless the horizontal dimension of each side of the cage is at least four times the length of the caged animal. The provisions of this subsection do not apply to the North Dakota state fair association, to agricultural fair associations, to any agricultural display of caged animals by any political subdivision, or to district, regional, or national educational livestock or poultry exhibitions. Zoos which have been approved by the health district or the governing body of the political subdivision which has jurisdiction over the zoos are exempt from the provisions of this subsection.

8. Repealed by S.L. 1975, ch. 106, s 397.

OHIO REVISED CODE § 959.13 CRUELTY TO ANIMALS.

(A) No person shall:

(1) Torture an animal, deprive one of necessary sustenance, unnecessarily or cruelly beat, needlessly mutilate or kill, or impound or

confine an animal without supplying it during such confinement with a sufficient quantity of good wholesome food and water;

(2) Impound or confine an animal without affording it, during such confinement, access to shelter from wind, rain, snow, or excessive direct sunlight if it can reasonably be expected that the animal would otherwise become sick or in some other way suffer. Division (A)(2) of this section does not apply to animals impounded or confined prior to slaughter. For the purpose of this section, shelter means a man-made enclosure, windbreak, sunshade, or natural windbreak or sunshade that is developed from the earth's contour, tree development, or vegetation.

(3) Carry or convey an animal in a cruel or inhuman manner;

(4) Keep animals other than cattle, poultry or fowl, swine, sheep, or goats in an enclosure without wholesome exercise and change of air, nor or [sic] feed cows on food that produces impure or unwholesome milk;

(5) Detain livestock in railroad cars or compartments longer than twenty-eight hours after they are so placed without supplying them with necessary food, water, and attention, nor permit such stock to be so crowded as to overlie, crush, wound, or kill each other.

(B) Upon the written request of the owner or person in custody of any particular shipment of livestock, which written request shall be separate and apart from any printed bill of lading or other railroad form, the length of time in which such livestock may be detained in any cars or compartments without food, water, and attention, may be extended to thirty-six hours without penalty therefor. This section does not prevent the dehorning of cattle.

(C) All fines collected for violations of this section shall be paid to the society or association for the prevention of cruelty to animals, if there be such in the county, township, or municipal corporation where such violation occurred.

OKLAHOMA STATUTES § 1685. CRUELTY TO ANIMALS.

Any person who shall willfully or maliciously overdrive, overload, torture, destroy or kill, or cruelly beat or injure, maim or mutilate, any animal in subjugation or captivity, whether wild or tame, and whether belonging to himself or to another, or deprive any such animal of necessary food, drink or shelter; or who shall cause, procure or permit any such animal to be so overdriven, overloaded, tortured, destroyed or killed, or cruelly beaten or injured, maimed or mutilated, or deprived of necessary food, drink or shelter; or who shall willfully set on foot, instigate, engage in, or in any way further any act of cruelty to any animal, or any act tending to produce such cruelty, shall be punished by imprisonment in the penitentiary not exceeding five (5) years, or by imprisonment in the county jail not exceeding one (1) year, or by fine not exceeding Five Hundred Dollars ($500.00); and any officer finding an animal so maltreated or abused shall cause the same to be taken care of, and the charges therefor shall be a lien upon such animal, to be collected thereon as upon a pledge or a lien.

1995 OREGON REVISED STATUTES § 167.315. ANIMAL ABUSE IN THE SECOND DEGREE.

(1) A person commits the crime of animal abuse in the second degree if, except as otherwise authorized by law, the person intentionally, knowingly or recklessly causes physical injury to an animal.

(2) Any practice of good animal husbandry is not a violation of this section.

(3) Animal abuse in the second degree is a Class B misdemeanor.

§ 167.320. Animal abuse in the first degree.

(1) A person commits the crime of animal abuse in the first degree if, except as otherwise authorized by law, the person intentionally, knowingly or recklessly:

(a) Causes serious physical injury to an animal; or

(b) Cruelly causes the death of an animal.

(2) Any practice of good animal husbandry is not a violation of this section.

(3) Animal abuse in the first degree is a Class A misdemeanor.

§ 167.322. Aggravated animal abuse in the first degree.

(1) A person commits the crime of aggravated animal abuse in the first degree if the person:

(a) Maliciously kills an animal; or

(b) Intentionally or knowingly tortures an animal.

(2) Aggravated animal abuse in the first degree is a Class C felony.

(3) As used in this section, "maliciously" means intentionally acting with a depravity of mind and reckless and wanton disregard of life.

§ 167.325. Animal neglect in the second degree.

(1) A person commits the crime of animal neglect in the second degree if, except as otherwise authorized by law, the person intentionally,

knowingly, recklessly or with criminal negligence fails to provide minimum care for an animal in such person's custody or control.

(2) Animal neglect in the second degree is a Class B misdemeanor.

§ 167.330. Animal neglect in the first degree.

(1) A person commits the crime of animal neglect in the first degree if, except as otherwise authorized by law, the person intentionally, knowingly, recklessly or with criminal negligence:

(a) Fails to provide minimum care for an animal in such person's custody or control; and

(b) Such failure to provide care results in serious physical injury or death to the animal.

(2) Animal neglect in the first degree is a Class A misdemeanor.

§ 167.335. Exemption from ORS 167.315 to 167.330.

Unless gross negligence can be shown, the provisions of ORS 167.315 to 167.330 shall not apply to:

(1) The treatment of livestock being transported by owner or common carrier;

(2) Animals involved in rodeos or similar exhibitions;

(3) Commercially grown poultry;

(4) Animals subject to good animal husbandry practices;

(5) The killing of livestock according to the provisions of ORS 603.065;

(6) Animals subject to good veterinary practices as described in ORS 686.030;

(7) Lawful fishing, hunting and trapping activities;

(8) Wildlife management practices under color of law; and

(9) Lawful scientific or agricultural research or teaching that involves the use of animals.

§ 167.340. Animal abandonment.

(1) A person commits the crime of animal abandonment if the person intentionally, knowingly, recklessly or with criminal negligence leaves a domesticated animal at a location without providing for the animal's continued care.

(2) It is no defense to the crime defined in subsection (1) of this section that the defendant abandoned the animal at or near an animal shelter,

veterinary clinic or other place of shelter if the defendant did not make reasonable arrangements for the care of the animal.

(3) Animal abandonment is a Class C misdemeanor.

PENNSYLVANIA STATUTES AND CONSOLIDATED STATUTES § 5511. CRUELTY TO ANIMALS.

(a) Killing, maiming or poisoning domestic animals or zoo animals, etc.—

(1) A person commits a misdemeanor of the second degree if he willfully and maliciously:

(i) Kills, maims or disfigures any domestic animal of another person or any domestic fowl of another person.

(ii) Administers poison to or exposes any poisonous substance with the intent to administer such poison to any domestic animal of another person or domestic fowl of another person.

(iii) Harasses, annoys, injures, attempts to injure, molests or interferes with a dog guide for an individual who is blind, a hearing dog for an individual who is deaf or audibly impaired or a service dog for an individual who is physically limited.

Any person convicted of violating the provisions of this paragraph shall be sentenced to pay a fine of not less than $500.

(2) A person commits a felony of the third degree if he willfully and maliciously:

(i) Kills, maims or disfigures any zoo animal in captivity.

(ii) Administers poison to or exposes any poisonous substance with the intent to administer such poison to any zoo animal in captivity.

2.1 (i) A person commits a misdemeanor of the second degree if he willfully and maliciously:

(A) Kills, maims, mutilates, tortures or disfigures any dog or cat, whether belonging to himself or otherwise.

(B) Administers poison to or exposes any poisonous substance with the intent to administer such poison to any dog or cat, whether belonging to himself or otherwise.

(ii) Any person convicted of violating the provisions of this paragraph shall be sentenced to pay a fine of not less than $1,000 or to imprisonment for not more than two years, or both. A subsequent conviction under this paragraph shall be a felony of the third degree. This paragraph shall apply to dogs and cats only.

(iii) The killing of a dog or cat by the owner of that animal is not malicious if it is accomplished in accordance with the act of December 22, 1983 (P.L. 303, No. 83), [FN1] referred to as the Animal Destruction Method Authorization Law.

(3) This subsection shall not apply to:

(i) the killing of any animal taken or found in the act of actually destroying any domestic animal or domestic fowl;

(ii) the killing of any animal or fowl pursuant to the act of June 3, 1937 (P.L. 1225, No. 316), [FN2] known as The Game Law, or Pa.C.S. ss 2384 (relating to declaring dogs public nuisances) and 2385 (relating to destruction of dogs declared public nuisances), or the regulations promulgated thereunder; or

(iii) such reasonable activity as may be undertaken in connection with vermin control or pest control.

(b) Regulating certain actions concerning fowl or rabbits.—A person commits a summary offense if he sells, offers for sale, barters, or gives away baby chickens, ducklings, or other fowl, under one month of age, or rabbits under two months of age, as pets, toys, premiums or novelties or if he colors, dyes, stains or otherwise changes the natural color of baby chickens, ducklings or other fowl, or rabbits or if he brings or transports the same into this Commonwealth. This section shall not be construed to prohibit the sale or display of such baby chickens, ducklings, or other fowl, or such rabbits, in proper facilities by persons engaged in the business of selling them for purposes of commercial breeding and raising.

(c) Cruelty to animals.—A person commits a summary offense if he wantonly or cruelly illtreats, overloads, beats, otherwise abuses any animal, or neglects any animal as to which he has a duty of care, whether belonging to himself or otherwise, or abandons any animal, or deprives any animal of necessary sustenance, drink, shelter or veterinary care, or access to clean and sanitary shelter which will protect the animal against inclement weather and preserve the animal's body heat and keep it dry. This subsection shall not apply to activity undertaken in normal agricultural operation.

(d) Selling or using disabled horse.—A person commits a summary offense if he offers for sale or sells any horse, which by reason of debility, disease or lameness, or for other cause, could not be worked or used without violating the laws against cruelty to animals, or leads, rides, drives or transports any such horse for any purpose, except that of conveying the horse to the nearest available appropriate facility for its humane keeping or destruction or for medical or surgical treatment.

(e) Transporting animals in cruel manner.—A person commits a summary offense if he carries, or causes, or allows to be carried in or upon any cart, or other vehicle whatsoever, any animal in a cruel or inhumane manner. The person taking him into custody may take charge of the animal and of any such vehicle and its contents, and deposit the same in some safe place of custody, and any necessary expenses which may be incurred for taking charge of and keeping the same, and sustaining any such animal, shall be a lien thereon, to be paid before the same can lawfully be recovered, or the said expenses or any part thereof remaining unpaid may be recovered by the person incurring the same from the owner of said creature in any action therefor.

For the purposes of this section, it shall not be deemed cruel or inhumane to transport live poultry in crates so long as not more than 15 pounds of live poultry are allocated to each cubic foot of space in the crate.

(f) Hours of labor of animals.—A person commits a summary offense if he leads, drives, rides or works or causes or permits any other person to lead, drive, ride or work any horse, mare, mule, ox, or any other animal, whether belonging to himself or in his possession or control, for more than 15 hours in any 24 hour period, or more than 90 hours in any one week.

Nothing in this subsection contained shall be construed to warrant any persons leading, driving, riding or walking any animal a less period than 15 hours, when so doing shall in any way violate the laws against cruelty to animals.

(g) Cruelty to cow to enhance appearance of udder.—A person commits a summary offense if he kneads or beats or pads the udder of any cow, or willfully allows it to go unmilked for a period of 24 hours or more, for the purpose of enhancing the appearance or size of the udder of said cow, or by a muzzle or any other device prevents its calf, if less than six weeks old, from obtaining nourishment, and thereby relieving the udder of said cow, for a period of 24 hours.

(h) Cropping ears of dog; prima facie evidence of violation.—A person commits a summary offense if he crops or cuts off, or causes or procures to be cropped or cut off, the whole, or part of the ear or ears of a dog or shows or exhibits or procures the showing or exhibition of any dog whose ear is or ears are cropped or cut off, in whole or in part, unless the person showing such dog has in his possession either a certificate of veterinarian stating that such cropping was done by the veterinarian or a certificate of registration from a county treasurer, showing that such dog was cut or cropped before this section became effective.

The provisions of this section shall not prevent a veterinarian from cutting or cropping the whole or part of the ear or ears of a dog when such dog is anesthetized, and shall not prevent any person from causing or procuring such cutting or cropping of a dog's ear or ears by a veterinarian.

The possession by any person of a dog with an ear or ears cut off or cropped and with the wound resulting therefrom unhealed, or any such dog being found in the charge or custody of any person or confined upon the premises owned by or under the control of any person, shall be prima facie evidence of a violation of this subsection by such person except as provided for in this subsection.

The owner of any dog whose ear or ears have been cut off or cropped before this section became effective may, if a resident of this Commonwealth, register such dog with the treasurer of the county where he resides, and if a nonresident of this Commonwealth, with the treasurer of any county of this Commonwealth, by certifying, under oath, that the ear or ears of such dog were cut or cropped before this section became effective, and the payment of a fee of $1 into the county treasury. The said treasurer shall thereupon issue to such person a certificate showing such dog to be a lawfully cropped dog.

(h.1) Animal fighting.—A person commits a felony of the third degree if he:

(1) for amusement or gain, causes, allows or permits any animal to engage in animal fighting;

(2) receives compensation for the admission of another person to any place kept or used for animal fighting;

(3) owns, possesses, keeps, trains, promotes, purchases or knowingly sells any animal for animal fighting;

(4) in any way knowingly encourages, aids or assists therein;

(5) wagers on the outcome of an animal fight;

(6) pays for admission to an animal fight or attends an animal fight as a spectator; or

(7) knowingly permits any place under his control or possession to be kept or used for animal fighting.

This subsection shall not apply to activity undertaken in a normal agricultural operation.

(i) Power to initiate criminal proceedings.—An agent of any society or association for the prevention of cruelty to animals, incorporated under the laws of the Commonwealth, shall have the same powers to initiate criminal proceedings provided for police officers by the Pennsylvania Rules of Criminal Procedure. An agent of any society or association for the prevention of cruelty to animals, incorporated under the laws of this Commonwealth, shall have standing to request any court of competent jurisdiction to enjoin any violation of this section.

(j) Seizure of animals kept or used for animal fighting.—Any police officer or agent of a society or association for the prevention of cruelty to animals incorporated under the laws of this Commonwealth, shall have power to seize any animal kept, used, or intended to be used for animal fighting. When the seizure is made, the animal or animals so seized shall not be deemed absolutely forfeited, but shall be held by the officer or agent seizing the same until a conviction of some person is first obtained for a violation of subsection (h.1). The officer or agent making such seizure shall make due return to the issuing authority, of the number and kind of animals or creatures so seized by him. Where an animal is thus seized, the police officer or agent is authorized to provide such care as is reasonably necessary, and where any animal thus seized is found to be disabled, injured or diseased beyond reasonable hope of recovery, the police officer or agent is authorized to provide for the humane destruction of the animal. In addition to any other penalty provided by law, the authority imposing sentence upon a conviction for any violation of subsection (h.1) shall order the forfeiture or surrender of any abused, neglected or deprived animal of the defendant to any society or association for the prevention of cruelty to animals duly incorporated under the laws of this Commonwealth and shall require that the owner pay the cost of the keeping, care and destruction of the animal.

(k) Killing homing pigeons.—A person commits a summary offense if he shoots, maims or kills any antwerp or homing pigeon, either while on flight or at rest, or detains or entraps any such pigeon which carries the name of its owner.

(l) Search warrants.—Where a violation of this section is alleged, any issuing authority may, in compliance with the applicable provisions of the Pennsylvania Rules of Criminal Procedure, issue to any police officer or any agent of any society or association for the prevention of cruelty to animals duly incorporated under the laws of this Commonwealth a search warrant authorizing the search of any building or any enclosure in which any violation of this section is occurring or has occurred, and authorizing the seizure of evidence of the violation including, but not limited to, the animals which were the subject of the violation. Where an animal thus seized is found to be neglected or starving, the police officer or agent is authorized to provide such care as is reasonably necessary, and where any animal thus seized is found to be disabled, injured or diseased beyond reasonable hope of recovery, the police officer or agent is authorized to provide for the humane destruction of the animal. The cost of the keeping, care and destruction of the animal shall be paid by the owner thereof and claims for the costs shall constitute a lien upon the animal. In addition to any other penalty provided by law, the authority imposing sentence upon a conviction for any violation of this section may require that the owner pay the cost of the keeping, care and destruction of the animal. No search warrant shall be issued based upon an alleged violation of this section which authorizes any police officer or agent or other person to enter upon or search premises where scientific research work is being conducted by, or under the supervision of, graduates of duly accredited scientific schools or where biological products are being produced for the care or prevention of disease.

(m) Forfeiture.—In addition to any other penalty provided by law, the authority imposing sentence upon a conviction for any violation of this section may order the forfeiture or surrender of any abused, neglected or deprived animal of the defendant to any society or association for the prevention of cruelty to animals duly incorporated under the laws of this Commonwealth.

(m.1) Fine for summary offense.—In addition to any other penalty provided by law, a person convicted of a summary offense under this section shall pay a fine of not less than $50 nor more than $750 or to imprisonment for not more than 90 days, or both.

(n) Skinning of and selling or buying pelts of dogs and cats.—A person commits a summary offense if he skins a dog or cat or offers for sale or exchange or offers to buy or exchange the pelt or pelts of any dog or cat.

(o) Representation of humane society by attorney.—Upon prior authorization and approval by the district attorney of the county in which the proceeding is held, an association or agent may be represented in any proceeding under this section by any attorney admitted to practice before the Supreme Court of Pennsylvania and in good standing. Attorney's fees shall be borne by the humane society or association which is represented.

(o.1) Construction of section.—The provisions of this section shall not supersede the act of December 7, 1982 (P.L. 784, No. 225), [FN3] known as the Dog Law.

(p) Applicability of section.—This section shall not apply to, interfere with or hinder any activity which is authorized or permitted pursuant to the act of June 3, 1937 (P.L.1225, No. 316), known as The Game Law or Title 34 (relating to game).

(q) Definitions.—As used in this section, the following words and phrases shall have the meanings given to them in this subsection:

"Animal fighting." Fighting or baiting any bull, bear, dog, cock or other creature.

"Audibly impaired." The inability to hear air conduction thresholds at an average of 40 decibels or greater in the better ear.

"Blind." Having a visual acuity of 20/200 or less in the better eye with correction or having a limitation of the field of vision such that the widest diameter of the visual field subtends an angular distance not greater than 20 degrees.

"Deaf." Totally impaired hearing or hearing with or without amplification which is so seriously impaired that the primary means of receiving spoken language is through other sensory input, including, but not limited to, lip reading, sign language, finger spelling or reading.

"Domestic animal." Any dog, cat, equine animal, bovine animal, sheep, goat or porcine animal.

"Domestic fowl." Any avis raised for food, hobby or sport.

"Normal agricultural operation." Normal activities, practices and procedures that farmers adopt, use or engage in year after year in the production and preparation for market of poultry, livestock and their products in the production and harvesting of agricultural, agronomic, horticultural, silvicultural and aquicultural crops and commodities.

"Physically limited." Having limited ambulation, including, but not limited to, a temporary or permanent impairment or condition that causes an individual to use a wheelchair or walk with difficulty or insecurity, affects sight or hearing to the extent that an individual is insecure or exposed to danger, causes faulty coordination or reduces mobility, flexibility, coordination or perceptiveness.

"Zoo animal." Any member of the class of mammalia, aves, amphibia or reptilia which is kept in a confined area by a public body or private individual for purposes of observation by the general public.

GENERAL LAWS OF RHODE ISLAND 1956§ 4-1-2 OVERWORK, MISTREATMENT, OR FAILURE TO FEED ANIMALS — "SHELTER" DEFINED.

(A) Whoever shall overdrive, overload, drive when overloaded, overwork, torture, torment, deprive of necessary sustenance, cruelly beat, mutilate or cruelly kill, or cause or procure to be so overdriven, overloaded, driven when overloaded, overworked, tortured, tormented, deprived of necessary sustenance, cruelly beaten, mutilated or cruelly killed, any animal, and whoever, having the charge or custody of any animal, either as owner or otherwise, shall inflict cruelty upon that animal, or shall willfully fail to provide that animal with proper food, drink, shelter or protection from the weather, shall, for every such offense, be imprisoned not exceeding eleven (11) months, or be fined not less than fifty dollars ($50.00) nor exceeding five hundred dollars ($500), or be both imprisoned and fined as aforesaid.

(B) Every owner, possessor or person having charge of any animal may upon conviction of a violation of this section be ordered to forfeit all rights to ownership of the animal to the animal control officer of the city or town in which the offense occurred or to a humane society which owns and operates the shelter which provided the subject animal shelter subsequent to any confiscation of said animal pursuant to this section.

(C) "Shelters", as used in this chapter, shall mean a structure used to house any animal, and which will provide sufficient protection from inclement elements for the health and well-being of the animal.

§ 4-1-3 Unnecessary cruelty.

Every owner, possessor or person having the charge or custody of any animal, who shall cruelly drive or work that animal when unfit for labor, or cruelly abandon that animal, or who shall carry that animal, or cause that animal to be carried, in or upon any vehicle or otherwise in a cruel or inhuman manner, or wilfully authorize or permit that animal to be subjected to unnecessary torture, suffering or cruelty of any kind, or who shall place or cause to have placed on any animal any substance that may produce irritation or pain, or that shall be declared a hazardous substance by the U.S. Food and Drug Administration or by the Rhode Island Department of Health, shall be punished for every such offense in the manner provided in § 4-1-2; provided however, that this section shall not be deemed to include any drug having curative and therapeutic effect for disease in animals and which is prepared and intended for veterinary use.

CODE OF LAWS OF SOUTH CAROLINA 1976 § 47-1-40. ILL-TREATMENT OF ANIMALS GENERALLY.

(A) Whoever overloads, overdrives, overworks, or ill-treats any animal, or deprives any animal of necessary sustenance or shelter, or inflicts unnecessary pain or suffering upon any animal, or causes these things to be done, for every offense is guilty of a misdemeanor and, upon conviction, must be punished by imprisonment not exceeding sixty days or by a fine of not less than one hundred dollars nor more than four hundred dollars for a first offense; by imprisonment not exceeding ninety days or by a fine not exceeding eight hundred dollars, or both, for a second offense; or by imprisonment not exceeding two years or by a fine not exceeding two thousand dollars, or both, for a third or subsequent offense. Notwithstanding any other provision of law, a first offense under this subsection shall be tried in magistrate's court.

(B) Whoever tortures, torments, needlessly mutilates, cruelly kills, or inflicts excessive or repeated unnecessary pain or suffering upon any animal or causes the acts to be done for any of the offenses is guilty of a misdemeanor and, upon conviction, must be punished by imprisonment of not less than one hundred eighty days and not to exceed two years and by a fine of five thousand dollars.

(C) This section does not apply to fowl, accepted animal husbandry practices of farm operations, the training of animals, the practice of veterinary medicine, or activity authorized by Title 50.

SOUTH DAKOTA CODIFIED LAWS§ 9-29-11 CRUELTY TO ANIMALS.

Every municipality shall have power to prohibit and punish cruelty to animals.

§ 40-1-1 Definition of terms.

Terms used in chapters 40-1 and 40-2, mean:

(1) "Abandonment," giving up with the intent of never again regaining one's interests in, or rights to, an animal other than placing ownership with a responsible party;

(2) "Animal," any mammal, bird, reptile, amphibian or fish, except humans;

(3) "Board," the South Dakota animal industry board;

(4) "Captive wild animal," any wild animal held in man-made confinement or physically altered to limit movement and facilitate capture;

(5) "Domestic animal," any animal that through long association with man, has been bred to a degree which has resulted in genetic changes affecting the temperament, color, conformation or other attributes of the species to an extent that makes it unique and different from wild individuals of its kind;

(6) "Exotic animal," any animal not occurring naturally in the United States either currently or historically;

(7) "Impoundment," taking physical control and custody of an animal;

(8) "Non-domestic animal," any animal that is not domestic;

(9) "Other livestock," any agricultural or commercial animal owned, bred or raised for profit, but not including dogs, cats, rabbits or other household pets;

(10) "Wild animal," any animal not in captivity, other than a domestic animal; and

(11) "Zoological animal," any animal in any zoo or intended to be used in a zoo.

§ 40-1-2. Overwork, torture, starving or cruelty to animal prohibited.

§ 40-1-2.2 Mistreatment, torture or cruelty of animals defined.

For the purposes of this chapter and chapter 40-2, the mistreatment, torture or cruelty of an animal is any act or omission whereby unnecessary, unjustifiable or unreasonable physical pain or suffering is caused, permitted or allowed to continue including acts of mutilation.

§40-1-2.3 Neglect defined.

For the purposes of this chapter and chapter 40-2, the neglect of an animal is the failure to provide food, water, protection from the elements, adequate sanitation, adequate facilities or care generally considered to be standard and accepted for an animal's health and well-being consistent with the species, breed, physical condition and type of animal.

§ 40-1-2.4 Inhumane treatment defined.

For the purposes of this chapter and chapter 40-2, the inhumane treatment of an animal is any act of mistreatment, torture, cruelty, neglect, abandonment, mutilation or inhumane slaughter of an animal that is not consistent with generally accepted training, use and husbandry procedures for the species, breed, physical condition and type of animal.

TENNESSEE CODE § 39-14-202 CRUELTY TO ANIMALS.

(a) A person commits an offense who intentionally or knowingly:

(1) Tortures, maims or grossly overworks an animal;

(2) Fails unreasonably to provide necessary food, water, care or shelter for an animal in the person's custody;

(3) Abandons unreasonably an animal in the person's custody;

(4) Transports or confines an animal in a cruel manner; or

(5) Inflicts burns, cuts, lacerations, or other injuries or pain, by any method, including blistering compounds, to the legs or hooves of horses in order to make them sore for any purpose including, but not limited to, competition in horse shows and similar events.

(b) It is a defense to prosecution under this section that the person was engaged in accepted veterinary practices, medical treatment by the owner or with the owner's consent, or bona fide experimentation for scientific research.

(c) Whenever any person is taken into custody by any officer for violation of subdivision (a)(4), the officer may take charge of the vehicle or conveyance, and its contents, used by the person to transport the animal. The officer shall deposit these items in a safe place for custody. Any necessary expense incurred for taking charge of and sustaining the same shall be a lien thereon, to be paid before the same can lawfully be recovered; or the expenses, or any part thereof, remaining unpaid may be recovered by the person incurring the same of the owners of the animal in an action therefor.

(d) In addition to the penalty imposed in subsection (f), the court making the sentencing determination for a person convicted under this section shall order the person convicted to surrender custody and forfeit the animal or animals whose treatment was the basis of the conviction. Custody shall be given to a humane society incorporated under the laws of this state. The court may prohibit the person convicted from having custody of other animals for any period of time the court determines to be reasonable, or impose any other reasonable restrictions on the person's custody of animals as necessary for the protection of the animals.

(e)(1) Nothing in this section shall be construed as prohibiting the owner of a farm animal or someone acting with the consent of the owner of such animal from engaging in usual and customary practices which are accepted by colleges of agriculture or veterinary medicine with respect to such animal.

(2) It is an offense for a person other than an officer, agent or member of a society described in s 39-14-210 to knowingly interfere with the performance of any such agricultural practices permitted by subdivision (e)(1).

(3) An offense under subdivision (e)(2) is a Class B misdemeanor.

(f) An offense under this section is a Class A misdemeanor.

TEXAS STATUTES AND CODES § 42.09. CRUELTY TO ANIMALS.

(a) A person commits an offense if he intentionally or knowingly:

(1) tortures or seriously overworks an animal;

(2) fails unreasonably to provide necessary food, care, or shelter for an animal in his custody;

(3) abandons unreasonably an animal in his custody;

(4) transports or confines an animal in a cruel manner;

(5) kills, injures, or administers poison to an animal, other than cattle, horses, sheep, swine, or goats, belonging to another without legal authority or the owner's effective consent;

(6) causes one animal to fight with another;

(7) uses a live animal as a lure in dog race training or in dog coursing on a racetrack; or

(8) trips a horse.

(b) It is a defense to prosecution under this section that the actor was engaged in bona fide experimentation for scientific research.

(c) For purposes of this section:

(1) "Animal" means a domesticated living creature and wild living creature previously captured. "Animal" does not include an uncaptured wild creature or a wild creature whose capture was accomplished by conduct at issue under this section.

(2) "Trip" means to use an object to cause a horse to fall or lose its balance.

(d) An offense under this section is a Class A misdemeanor.

(e) It is a defense to prosecution under Subsection (a)(5) that the animal was discovered on the person's property in the act of or immediately after injuring or killing the person's goats, sheep, cattle, horses, swine, or poultry and that the person killed or injured the animal at the time of this discovery.

(f) It is a defense to prosecution under Subsection (a)(8) that the actor tripped the horse for the purpose of identifying the ownership of the horse or giving veterinary care to the horse.

UTAH CODE, 1953 § 76-9-301 CRUELTY TO ANIMALS.

(1) A person is guilty of cruelty to animals if the person intentionally, knowingly, recklessly, or with criminal negligence:

(a) fails to provide necessary food, care, or shelter for an animal in his custody;

(b) abandons an animal in the person's custody;

(c) transports or confines an animal in a cruel manner;

(d) injures an animal;

(e) causes any animal, not including a dog, to fight with another animal of like kind for amusement or gain; or

(f) causes any animal, including a dog, to fight with a different kind of animal or creature for amusement or gain.

(2) A violation of Subsection (1) is:

(a) a class B misdemeanor if committed intentionally or knowingly; and

(b) a class C misdemeanor if committed recklessly or with criminal negligence.

(3) A person is guilty of aggravated cruelty to an animal if the person:

(a) tortures an animal;

(b) administers poison or poisonous substances to an animal without having a legal privilege to do so;

(c) kills or causes to be killed an animal without having a legal privilege to do so.

(4) A violation of Subsection (3) is:

(a) a class A misdemeanor if committed intentionally or knowingly;

(b) a class B misdemeanor if committed recklessly; and

(c) a class C misdemeanor if committed with criminal negligence.

(5) It is a defense to prosecution under this section that the conduct of the actor towards the animal was:

(a) by a licensed veterinarian using accepted veterinary practice;

(b) directly related to bona fide experimentation for scientific research, provided that if the animal is to be destroyed, the manner employed will not be unnecessarily cruel unless directly necessary to the veterinary purpose or scientific research involved;

(c) permitted under Section 18-1-3;

(d) by a person who humanely destroys any animal found suffering past recovery for any useful purpose; or

(e) by a person who humanely destroys any apparently abandoned animal found on the person's property.

(6) For purposes of Subsection (5)(d), before destroying the suffering animal, the person who is not the owner of the animal shall obtain:

(a) the judgment of a veterinarian of the animal's nonrecoverable condition;

(b) the judgment of two other persons called by the person to view the unrecoverable condition of the animal in the person's presence;

(c) the consent from the owner of the animal to the destruction of the animal; or

(d) a reasonable conclusion that the animal's suffering is beyond recovery, through the person's own observation, if the person is in a location or circumstance where the person is unable to contact another person.

(7) This section does not affect or prohibit the training, instruction, and grooming of animals, so long as the methods used are in accordance with accepted husbandry practices.

(8)(a) This section does not affect or prohibit the use of an electronic locating or training collar by the owner of an animal for the purpose of lawful animal training, lawful hunting practices, or protecting against loss of that animal.

(b) County and municipal governments may not prohibit the use of an electronic locating or training collar.

(9) Upon conviction under this section, the court may in its discretion, in addition to other penalties:

(a) order the defendant to be evaluated to determine the need for psychiatric or psychological counseling, to receive counseling as the court determines to be appropriate, and to pay the costs of the evaluation and counseling;

(b) require the defendant to forfeit any rights the defendant has to the animal subjected to a violation of this section and to repay the reasonable costs incurred by any person or agency in caring for each animal subjected to violation of this section;

(c) order the defendant to no longer possess or retain custody of any animal, as specified by the court, during the period of the defendant's probation or parole or other period as designated by the court; and

(d) order the animal to be placed for the purpose of adoption or care in the custody of a county and municipal animal control agency, an animal welfare agency registered with the state, sold at public auction, or humanely destroyed.

(10) This section does not prohibit the use of animals in lawful training.

(11) As used in this section:

(a) "Abandons" means to intentionally deposit, leave, or drop off any live animal:

(i) without providing for the care of that animal; or

(ii) in a situation where conditions present an immediate, direct, and serious threat to the life, safety, or health of the animal.

(b) (i) "Animal" means a live, nonhuman vertebrate creature.

(ii) "Animal" does not include animals kept or owned for agricultural purposes and cared for in accordance with accepted husbandry practices, animals used for rodeo purposes, and does not include protected and unprotected wildlife as defined in Section 23-13-2.

(c) "Custody" means ownership, possession, or control over an animal.

(d) "Legal privilege" means an act authorized by state law, including Division of Wildlife Resources statutes and rules, and conducted in conformance with local ordinances.

(e) "Necessary food, care, and shelter" means appropriate and essential food and other needs of the animal, including veterinary care, and adequate protection against extreme weather conditions.

VERMONT STATUTES § 352. CRUELTY TO ANIMALS.

(a) A person commits the crime of cruelty to animals if the person:

(1) intentionally kills any animal belonging to another person without first obtaining legal authority or consent of the owner, or at-

tempts to kill or kills an animal with or without the owner's consent by a means causing undue suffering;

(2) overworks, overloads, tortures, torments, abandons, administers poison to, cruelly beats or mutilates an animal, exposes a poison with intent that it be taken by an animal;

(3) ties, tethers, or restrains an animal, either a pet or livestock, in a manner that is inhumane or is detrimental to its welfare. Accepted agricultural methods are exempted;

(4) deprives an animal which a person owns, possesses or acts as an agent for, of adequate food, water, shelter, rest or sanitation, or necessary medical attention, or transports an animal in overcrowded vehicles;

(5) owns, possesses, keeps or trains an animal engaged in an exhibition of fighting, or possesses, keeps or trains any animal with intent that it be engaged in an exhibition of fighting, or permits any such act to be done on premises under his or her charge or control;

(6) acts as judge or spectator at events of animal fighting or bets or wagers on the outcome of such fight;

(7) as poundkeeper, officer, agent of a humane society or as an owner or employee of an establishment for treatment, board or care of an animal, knowingly receives, sells, transfers or otherwise conveys an animal in his or her care for the purpose of research or vivisection;

(8) intentionally torments or harasses an animal owned or engaged by a police department or public agency of the state or its political subdivisions, or interferes with the lawful performance of a police animal;

(9) knowingly sells, offers for sale, barters or displays living baby chicks, ducklings or other fowl which have been dyed, colored or otherwise treated so as to impart to them an artificial color, or fails to provide poultry with proper brooder facilities;

(10) fails to ensure that a crate or other container used to transport, hold or ship in commerce live poultry is maintained in sanitary condition and so constructed as to provide sufficient ventilation and warmth; or

(11) uses a live animal as bait or lure in a race, game or contest, or in training animals in a manner inconsistent with Part 4 of Title 10 or the rules adopted thereunder.

(b) Except as provided in subsection (c) of this section, an affirmative defense to prosecution may be raised under this section when:

(1) except for vivisection or research under subdivision (a)(7) of this section, the defendant was a veterinarian whose conduct conformed to accepted veterinary practice for the area, or was a scientist whose conduct was a part of scientific research governed by accepted procedural standards subject to review by an institutional care and use committee;

(2) the defendant's conduct was designed to control or eliminate rodents, ants or other common pests on the defendant's own property;

(3) the defendant was a person appropriately licensed to utilize pesticides under chapter 87 of Title 6;

(4) the defendant humanely euthanized any animal as a representative of a duly organized humane society, animal shelter or town pound according to rules of this subchapter, or as a veterinarian destroying animals under chapter 193 or sections 3511 and 3513 of Title 20; or

(5) a state agency was implementing a rabies control program.

(c) An affirmative defense to a charge of abandonment under this section shall not be recognized where a person abandons an animal at or near an animal shelter or veterinary clinic, or other place of shelter, without making reasonable arrangements for the care of the animal.

(d) The authority to enforce this chapter shall not be construed in a manner inconsistent with the animal control or disease control eradication programs in Title 6, or chapters 191, 193, 194 and 195 of Title 20 or the provisions of Part 4 of Title 10, or the rules adopted thereunder.

CODE OF VIRGINIA § 3.1-796.122 CRUELTY TO ANIMALS; PENALTY.

A. Any person who—

(i) overrides, overdrives, overloads, tortures, ill-treats, abandons, willfully inflicts inhumane injury or pain not connected with bona fide scientific or medical experimentation, or cruelly or unnecessarily beats, maims, mutilates, or kills any animal, whether belonging to himself or another; or

(ii) deprives any animal of necessary sustenance, food, drink or shelter; or

(iii) willfully sets on foot, instigates, engages in, or in any way furthers any act of cruelty to any animal; or

(iv) carries or causes to be carried in or upon any vehicle, vessel or otherwise any animal in a cruel, brutal, or inhumane manner, so as to produce torture or unnecessary suffering; or

(v) causes any of the above things, or being the owner of such animal permits such acts to be done by another, shall be guilty of a Class 1 misdemeanor. Prosecution for violations of this subsection shall commence within five years after commission of the offense. Prosecutions of this subsection regarding agricultural animals, as defined in s 3.1-796.66, shall commence within one year after commission of the offense.

B. Any person who abandons any dog, cat or other domesticated animal in any public place including the right-of-way of any public highway, road or street or on the property of another shall be guilty of a Class 3 misdemeanor.

C. Nothing in this section shall be construed to prohibit the dehorning of cattle.

D. For the purposes of this section and ss 3.1-796.109, 3.1-796.111, 3.1- 796.113 through 3.1-796.115, and 3.1-796.125, the word animal shall be construed to include birds and fowl.

REVISED CODE OF WASHINGTON § 16.52.205. ANIMAL CRUELTY IN THE FIRST DEGREE.

A person is guilty of animal cruelty in the first degree when, except as authorized in law, he or she intentionally—

(a) inflicts substantial pain on,

(b) causes physical injury to, or

(c) kills an animal by a means causing undue suffering, or forces a minor to inflict unnecessary pain, injury, or death on an animal.

Animal cruelty in the first degree is a class C felony.

§ 16.52.207. Animal cruelty in the second degree.

(1) A person is guilty of animal cruelty in the second degree if, under circumstances not amounting to first degree animal cruelty, the person knowingly, recklessly, or with criminal negligence inflicts unnecessary suffering or pain upon an animal.

(2) An owner of an animal is guilty of animal cruelty in the second degree if, under circumstances not amounting to first degree animal cruelty, the owner knowingly, recklessly, or with criminal negligence:

(a) Fails to provide the animal with necessary food, water, shelter, rest, sanitation, ventilation, space, or medical attention and the animal suffers unnecessary or unjustifiable physical pain as a result of the failure; or

(b) Abandons the animal.

(3) Animal cruelty in the second degree is a misdemeanor.

(4) In any prosecution of animal cruelty in the second degree, it shall be an affirmative defense, if established by the defendant by a preponderance of the evidence, that the defendant's failure was due to economic distress beyond the defendant's control.

WEST VIRGINIA CODE 1966 § 19-20-12 DOGS, OTHER ANIMALS AND REPTILES PROTECTED BY LAW; UNLAWFUL KILLING THEREOF; AGGRIEVED OWNER'S REMEDY; PENALTIES; PENALTIES FOR UNLAWFUL STEALING OF PETS.

(a) Any dog which is registered, kept and controlled as provided in this article or any dog, cat, other animal or any reptile which is owned, kept and maintained as a pet by any person, irrespective of age, shall be protected by law; and any person who shall intentionally and unlawfully kill, injure or poison any such dog, cat, other animal or any reptile as specified above, or shall, in any other manner, intentionally and unlawfully cause the death or injury of any such dog, cat, other animal or any reptile shall be guilty of a misdemeanor, and, upon conviction thereof, shall be ordered to provide public service for not less than thirty nor more than ninety days, or fined not more than three hundred dollars, or both. Any person whose dog, cat, other animal or reptile as specified herein shall be killed or injured wrongfully or unlawfully by any other person shall have a right of action against the person who shall so kill or injure such dog, cat, animal or reptile but in no case involving a dog can recovery be had in excess of the assessed value of such dog.

(b) Any person who shall intentionally and unlawfully steal a dog, cat, other animal or reptile as specified in subsection (a) of this section, shall be guilty of a misdemeanor, and, upon conviction thereof, shall be ordered to provide public service for not less than thirty nor more than ninety days or fined not less than three hundred nor more than five hundred dollars, or both. Any person violating the provisions of this subsection shall, for the second or subsequent offense, be guilty of a misdemeanor, and, upon conviction thereof, shall be confined in the county jail for a period of not less than ninety days nor more than six months, or shall be ordered to provide public service for not more than one year, and fined not less than five hundred nor more than one thousand dollars. In no case can any action or prosecution relating to a dog under the provisions of this section be maintained if the dog concerned shall not have been duly registered pursuant to the provisions of this article or owned and kept pursuant to the provisions of this section or owned and kept pursuant to the provisions of this section at the time the cause of action shall have arisen.

(c) The commissioner of agriculture is hereby authorized to designate such reasonable number of his present employees as may be necessary to investigate alleged incidents of the unlawful stealing of dogs, other domestic animals or reptiles, alleged incidents of cruelty to such animals or reptiles and the alleged incidents of the unlawful stealing of such animals or reptiles for the purpose of sale to medical or other research companies. Such deputies shall make the results of their investigations known to any law-enforcement officers who have authority to enforce the provisions of this article.

(d) It shall be the duty of all members of the department of public safety, sheriffs and police officers to aid in the enforcement of the provisions of this article, and, for services rendered in the enforcement thereof, such persons shall be entitled to fees in the amounts set forth in section eight [s 19-20-8]. Such fees shall be paid by the county commission from the dog and kennel fund.

WISCONSIN STATUTES § 951.02. MISTREATING ANIMALS.

No person may treat any animal, whether belonging to the person or another, in a cruel manner. This section does not prohibit bona fide experiments carried on for scientific research or normal and accepted veterinary practices.

WYOMING STATUTES 1977 § 6-3-203 CRUELTY TO ANIMALS; PENALTIES; LIMITATION ON MANNER OF DESTRUCTION.

(a) A person commits cruelty to animals if, without lawful authority, he knowingly:

(i) Overrides, overdrives, overloads, drives when overloaded, overworks, tortures or torments an animal or deprives an animal of necessary sustenance;

(ii) Unnecessarily or cruelly beats, injures, mutilates or kills an animal; or

(iii) Carries an animal in a cruel or inhumane manner.

(b) A person commits cruelty to animals if he has the charge and custody of any animal and unnecessarily fails to provide it with the proper food, drink or protection from the weather, or cruelly abandons the animal, or in the case of immediate, obvious, serious illness or injury, fails to provide the animal with appropriate care.

(c) A person commits aggravated cruelty to animals if he:

(i) Repealed by Laws 1987, ch. 91, s 2.

(ii) Owns, possesses, keeps or trains fowls or dogs with the intent to allow the dog or fowl to engage in an exhibition of fighting with another dog or fowl;

(iii) Repealed by Laws 1987, ch. 91, s 2.

(iv) For gain causes or allows any dog or fowl to fight with another dog or fowl;

(v) Knowingly permits any act prohibited under paragraphs (ii) or @P1 = (iv) of this subsection on any premises under his charge or control; or

(vi) Promotes any act prohibited under paragraphs (ii) or (iv) of this subsection.

(d) A person shall not destroy an animal by the use of a high-altitude decompression chamber or a carbon monoxide gas chamber utilizing a gasoline engine. This subsection is uniformly applicable to all cities and towns.

(e) Cruelty to animals is a misdemeanor punishable by imprisonment for not more than six (6) months, a fine of not more than seven hundred fifty dollars ($750.00), or both except that a subsequent offense, or aggravated cruelty to animals as defined by paragraphs (c)(ii), (iv), (v) and (vi) of this section is a high misdemeanor punishable by not more than one (1) year imprisonment, a fine of not more than five thousand dollars ($5,000.00), or both.

(f) Nothing in subsection (c) of this section may be construed to prohibit:

(i) The use of dogs in the management of livestock by the owner of the livestock, his employees or agents or other persons in lawful custody of the livestock;

(ii) The use of dogs or raptors in hunting; or

(iii) The training of dogs or raptors or the use of equipment in the training of dogs or raptors for any purpose not prohibited by law;

(iv) A person from humanely destroying an animal;

(v) The use of commonly accepted agricultural and livestock practices on livestock; or

(vi) Rodeo events, whether the event is performed in a rodeo, jackpot or otherwise.

(g) A person commits cruelty to animals if he is knowingly present at any place where an exhibition of fighting of fowls or dogs is occurring for amusement or gain.

(h) If a person convicted of cruelty to animals under this section is also the owner of the animal, the court may require the person to forfeit ownership of the animal to the county in which the person is convicted. This subsection shall not affect the interest of any secured party or other person who has not participated in the offense.

(j) In addition to any sentence and penalties imposed under subsections (e) and (h) of this section, the court may:

(i) Require the defendant to pay all reasonable costs incurred in providing necessary food and water, veterinary attention and treatment for any animal affected; and

(ii) Prohibit or limit the defendant's ownership, possession or custody of animals, as the court deems appropriate.

(k) Each animal affected by the defendant's conduct may constitute a separate count for the purposes of prosecution, conviction, sentencing and penalties under this section.

APPENDIX 16:
THE HORSE PROTECTION ACT (15 U.S.C. §§ 1821 1831)

SECTION 1.

This Act may be cited as the "Horse Protection Act."

SECTION 2.

As used in this Act unless the context otherwise requires:

(1) The term "management" means any person who organizes, exercises control over, or administers or who is responsible for organizing, directing, or administering.

(2) The term "Secretary" means the Secretary of Agriculture.

(3) The term "sore" when used to describe a horse means that —

(A) an irritating or blistering agent has been applied, internally or externally, by a person to any limb of a horse,

(B) any burn, cut, or laceration has been inflicted by a person on any limb of a horse,

(C) any tack, nail, screw, or chemical agent has been injected by a person into or used by a person on any limb of a horse, or

(D) any other substance or device has been used by a person on any limb of a horse or a person has engaged in a practice involving a horse, and, as a result of such application, infliction, injection, use, or practice, such horse suffers, or can reasonably be expected to suffer, physical pain or distress, inflammation, or lameness when walking, trotting, or otherwise moving, except that such term does not include such an application, infliction, injection, use, or practice in connection with the therapeutic treatment of a horse by or under the supervision of a person licensed to practice veterinary medicine in the State in which such treatment was given.

(4) The term "State" means any of the several States, the District of Columbia, the Commonwealth of Puerto Rico, the Virgin Islands, Guam, American Samoa, and the Trust Territory of the Pacific Islands.

SECTION 3

The Congress finds and declares that—

(1) the soring of horses is cruel and inhumane;

(2) horses shown or exhibited which are sore, where such soreness improves the performance of such horse, compete unfairly with horses which are not sore;

(3) the movement, showing, exhibition, or sale of sore horses in intrastate commerce adversely affects and burdens interstate and foreign commerce;

(4) all horses which are subject to regulation under this Act are either in interstate or foreign commerce or substantially affect such commerce; and

(5) regulation under this Act by the Secretary is appropriate to prevent and eliminate burdens upon commerce and to effectively regulate commerce.

SECTION 4.

(a) The management of any horse show or horse exhibition shall disqualify any horse from being shown or exhibited (1) which is sore or (2) if the management has been notified by a person appointed in accordance with regulations under subsection (c) of this section or by the Secretary that the horse is sore.

(b) The management of any horse sale or auction shall prohibit the sale or auction or exhibition for the purpose of sale of any horse (1) which is sore or (2) if the management has been notified by a person appointed in accordance with regulations under subsection © or by the Secretary that the horse is sore.

(c) The Secretary shall prescribe by regulation requirements for the appointment by the management of any horse show, horse exhibition, or horse sale or auction of persons qualified to detect and diagnose a horse which is sore or to otherwise inspect horses for the purposes of enforcing this Act. Such requirements shall prohibit the appointment of persons who, after notice and opportunity for a hearing, have been disqualified by the Secretary to make such detection, diagnosis, or inspection. Appointment of a person in accordance with the requirements prescribed under this subsection shall not be construed as authorizing such person to conduct inspections in a manner other than that prescribed for inspections by the Secretary (or the Secretary's representative) under subsection (e).

(d) The management of a horse show, horse exhibition, or horse sale or auction shall establish and maintain such records, make such reports, and provide such information as the Secretary may by regulation reasonably require for the purposes of implementing this Act or to determine compliance with this Act. Upon request of an officer or employee duly designated by the Secretary, such management shall permit entry at all reasonable times for the inspection and copying (on or off the premises) of records required to be maintained under this subsection.

(e) For purposes of enforcement of this Act (including any regulation promulgated under this Act) the Secretary, or any representative of the Secretary duly designated by the Secretary, may inspect any horse show, horse exhibition, or horse sale or auction or any horse at any such show, exhibition, sale, or auction. Such an inspection may only be made upon presenting appropriate credentials. Each such inspection shall be commenced and completed with reasonable promptness and shall be conducted within reasonable limits and in a reasonable manner. An inspection under this subsection shall extend to all things (including records) bearing on whether the requirements of this Act have been complied with.

SECTION 5. THE FOLLOWING CONDUCT IS PROHIBITED:

(1) The shipping, transporting, moving, delivering, or receiving of any horse which is sore with reason to believe that such horse while it is sore may be shown, exhibited, entered for the purpose of being shown or exhibited, sold, auctioned, or offered for sale, in any horse show, horse exhibition, or horse sale or auction; except that this paragraph does not apply to the shipping, transporting, moving, delivering, or receiving of any horse by a common or contract carrier or an employee thereof in the usual course of the carrier's business or employee's employment unless the carrier or employee has reason to believe that such horse is sore.

(2) The (A) showing or exhibiting, in any horse show or horse exhibition, of any horse which is sore, (B) entering for the purpose of showing or exhibiting in any horse show or horse exhibition, any horse which is sore, (C) selling, auctioning, or offering for sale, in any horse sale or auction, any horse which is sore, and (D) allowing any activity

described in clause (A), (B), or (C) respecting a horse which is sore by the owner of such horse.

(3) The failure by the management of any horse show or horse exhibition, which does not appoint and retain a person in accordance with section 1823(c) of this title, to disqualify from being shown or exhibited any horse which is sore.

(4) The failure by the management of any horse sale or auction, which does not appoint and retain a qualified person in accordance with section 1823(c) of this title, to prohibit the sale, offering for sale, or auction of any horse which is sore.

(5) The failure by the management of any horse show or horse exhibition, which has appointed and retained a person in accordance with section 1823(c) of this title, to disqualify from being shown or exhibited any horse (A) which is sore, and (B) after having been notified by such person or the Secretary that the horse is sore or after otherwise having knowledge that the horse is sore.

(6) The failure by the management of any horse sale or auction which has appointed and retained a person in accordance with section 1823(c) of this title, to prohibit the sale, offering for sale, or auction of any horse (A) which is sore, and (B) after having been notified by such person or the Secretary or after otherwise having knowledge that the horse is sore.

(7) The showing or exhibiting at a horse show or horse exhibition; the selling or auctioning at a horse sale or auction; the allowing to be shown, exhibited, or sold at a horse show, horse exhibition, or horse sale or auction; the entering for the purpose of showing or exhibiting in any horse show or horse exhibition; or offering for sale at a horse sale or auction, any horse which is wearing or bearing any equipment, device, paraphernalia, or substance which the Secretary by regulation under section 1828 of this title prohibits to prevent the soring of horses.

(8) The failing to establish, maintain, or submit records, notices, reports, or other information required under section 1823 of this title.

(9) The failure or refusal to permit access to or copying of records, or the failure or refusal to permit entry or inspection, as required by section 1823 of this title.

(10) The removal of any marking required by the Secretary to identify a horse as being detained.

(11) The failure or refusal to provide the Secretary with adequate space or facilities, as the Secretary may by regulation under section 1828 of

this title prescribe, in which to conduct inspections or any other activity authorized to be performed by the Secretary under this Act.

SECTION 6.

(a) (1) Except as provided in paragraph (2) of this subsection, any person who knowingly violates section 1824 of this title shall, upon conviction thereof, be fined not more than $3,000, or imprisoned for not more than one year, or both.

(a) (2) (A) If any person knowingly violates section 1824 of this title, after one or more prior convictions of such person for such a violation have become final, such person shall, upon conviction thereof, be fined not more than $5,000, or imprisoned for not more than two years, or both.

(a) (2) (B) Any person who knowingly makes, or causes to be made, a false entry or statement in any report required under this Act; who knowingly makes, or causes to be made, any false entry in any account, record, or memorandum required to be established and maintained by any person or in any notification or other information required to be submitted to the Secretary under section 1823 of this title; who knowingly neglects or fails to make or cause to be made, full, true, and correct entries in such accounts, records, memoranda, notification, or other materials; who knowingly removes any such documentary evidence out of the jurisdiction of the United States; who knowingly mutilates, alters, or by any other means falsifies any such documentary evidence; or who knowingly refuses to submit any such documentary evidence to the Secretary for inspection and copying shall be guilty of an offense against the United States, and upon conviction thereof shall be fined not more than $5,000, or imprisoned for not more than three years, or both.

(a) (2) (C) Any person who forcibly assaults, resists, opposes, impedes, intimidates, or interferes with any person while engaged in or on account of the performance of his official duties under this Act shall be fined not more than $5,000, or imprisoned not more than three years, or both. Whoever, in the commission of such acts, uses a deadly or dangerous weapon shall be fined not more than $10,000, or imprisoned not more than ten years, or both. Whoever kills any person while engaged in or on account of the performance of his official duties under this Act shall be punishable as provided under sections 1111 and 1112 of title 18.

(b) (1) Any person who violates section 1824 of this title shall be liable to the United States for a civil penalty of not more than $2,000 for each violation. No penalty shall be assessed unless such person is given notice and opportunity for a hearing before the Secretary with respect to such violation. The amount of such civil penalty shall be assessed by the Secretary by written order. In determining the amount of such penalty, the Secretary shall take into account all factors relevant to such determination, including the nature, circumstances, extent, and gravity of the prohibited conduct and, with respect to the person found to have engaged in such conduct, the degree of culpability, any history of prior offenses, ability to pay, effect on ability to continue to do business, and such other matters as justice may require.

(b) (2) Any person against whom a violation is found and a civil penalty assessed under paragraph (1) of this subsection may obtain review in the court of appeals of the United States for the circuit in which such person resides or has his place of business or in the United States Court of Appeals for the District of Columbia Circuit by filing a notice of appeal in such court within 30 days from the date of such order and by simultaneously sending a copy of such notice by certified mail to the Secretary. The Secretary shall promptly file in such court a certified copy of the record upon which such violation was found and such penalty assessed, as provided in section 2112 of title 28. The findings of the Secretary shall be set aside if found to be unsupported by substantial evidence.

(b) (3) If any person fails to pay an assessment of a civil penalty after it has become a final and unappealable order, or after the appropriate court of appeals has entered final judgment in favor of the Secretary, the Secretary shall refer the matter to the Attorney General, who shall recover the amount assessed in any appropriate district court of the United States. In such action, the validity and appropriateness of the final order imposing the civil penalty shall not be subject to review.

(b) (4) The Secretary may, in his discretion, compromise, modify, or remit, with or without conditions, any civil penalty assessed under this subsection.

(c) In addition to any fine, imprisonment, or civil penalty authorized under this section, any person who was convicted under subsection (a) of this section or who paid a civil penalty assessed under subsection (b) of this section or is subject to a final order under such subsection assessing a civil penalty for any violation of any provision of this Act or any regulation issued under this Act may be disqualified by order of the Secretary, after notice and an opportunity for a hearing before the Secretary, from showing or exhibiting any horse, judging or managing any horse show, horse exhibition, or horse sale or auction for a period of not less than one year for the first violation and not less than five years for any subsequent violation. Any person who knowingly fails to obey an order of disqualification shall be subject to a civil penalty of not more than $3,000 for each violation. Any horse show, horse exhibition, or horse sale or auction, or the management thereof, collectively and severally, which knowingly allows any person who is under an order of disqualification to show or exhibit any horse, to enter for the purpose of showing or exhibiting any horse, to take part in managing or judging, or otherwise to participate in any horse show, horse exhibition, or horse sale or auction in violation of an order shall be subject to a civil penalty of not more than $3,000 for each violation. The provisions of subsection (b) of this section respecting the assessment, review, collection, and compromise, modification, and remission of a civil penalty apply with respect to civil penalties under this subsection.

(d) (1) The Secretary may require by subpoena the attendance and testimony of witnesses and the production of books, papers, and documents relating to any matter under investigation or the subject of a proceeding. Witnesses summoned before the Secretary shall be paid the same fees and mileage that are paid witnesses in the courts of the United States.

(d) (2) The attendance of witnesses, and the production of books, papers, and documents, may be required at any designated place from any place in the United States. In case of disobedience to a subpoena the Secretary, or any party to a proceeding before the Secretary, may invoke the aid of any appropriate district court of the United States in requiring attendance and testimony of witnesses and the production of such books, papers, and documents under the provisions of this Act.

(d) (3) The Secretary may order testimony to be taken by deposition under oath in any proceeding or investigation pending before him, at any stage of the proceeding or investigation. Depositions may be taken before any person designated by the Secretary who has power to administer oaths. The Secretary may also require the production of books, papers, and documents at the taking of depositions.

(d) (4) Witnesses whose depositions are taken and the persons taking them shall be entitled to the same fees as paid for like services in the courts of the United States or in other jurisdictions in which they may appear.

(d) (5) In any civil or criminal action to enforce this Act or any regulation under this Act a horse shall be presumed to be a horse which is sore if it manifests abnormal sensitivity or inflammation in both of its forelimbs or both of its hind limbs.

(d) (6) The United States district courts, the District Court of Guam, the District Court of the Virgin Islands, the highest court of American Samoa, and the United States courts of the other territories, are vested with jurisdiction specifically to enforce, and to prevent and restrain violations of this Act, and shall have jurisdiction in all other kinds of cases arising under this Act, except as provided in subsection (b) of this section.

(e) (1) The Secretary may detain (for a period not to exceed twenty-four hours) for examination, testing, or the taking of evidence, any horse at any horse show, horse exhibition, or horse sale or auction which is sore or which the Secretary has probable cause to believe is sore. The Secretary may require the temporary marking of any horse during the period of its detention for the purpose of identifying the horse as detained. A horse which is detained subject to this paragraph shall not be moved by any person from the place it is so detained except as authorized by the Secretary or until the expiration of the detention period applicable to the horse.

(e) (2) Any equipment, device, paraphernalia, or substance which was used in violation of any provision of this Act or any regulation issued under this Act or which contributed to the soring of any horse at or prior to any horse show, horse exhibition, or horse sale or auction, shall be liable to be proceeded against, by process of libel for the seizure and condemnation of such equipment, device, paraphernalia, or substance, in any United States district court within the jurisdiction of which such equipment, device, paraphernalia, or substance is found. Such proceedings shall conform as nearly as possible to proceedings in rem in admiralty.

SECTION 7.

Whenever the Secretary believes that a willful violation of this Act has occurred and that prosecution is needed to obtain compliance with this Act, he shall inform the Attorney General and the Attorney General shall take such action with respect to such matter as he deems appropriate.

SECTION 8.

(a) The Secretary, in carrying out the provisions of this Act, shall utilize, to the maximum extent practicable, the existing personnel and facilities of the Department of Agriculture. The Secretary is further authorized to utilize the officers and employees of any State, with its consent, and with or without reimbursement, to assist him in carrying out the provisions of this Act.

(b) The Secretary may, upon request, provide technical and other nonfinancial assistance (including the lending of equipment on such terms and conditions as the Secretary determines is appropriate) to any State to assist it in administering and enforcing any law of such State designed to prohibit conduct described in section 5.

SECTION 9.

The Secretary is authorized to issue such rules and regulations as he deems necessary to carry out the provisions of this Act.

SECTION 10.

No provision of this Act shall be construed as indicating an intent on the part of the Congress to occupy the field in which such provision operates to the exclusion of the law of any State on the same subject matter, unless there is a direct and positive conflict between such provision and the law of the State so that the two cannot be reconciled or consistently stand together. Nor shall any provision of this Act be construed to exclude the Federal Government from enforcing the provision of this Act within any State, whether or not such State has enacted legislation on the same subject, it being the intent of the Congress to establish concurrent jurisdiction with the States over such subject matter. In no case shall any such State take any action pursuant to this section involving a violation of any such law of that State which would preclude the United States from enforcing the provisions of this Act against any person.

SECTION 11.

On or before the expiration of thirty calendar months following the date of enactment of this Act, and every twelve months thereafter, the Secretary shall submit to the Congress a report upon the matters covered by this Act, including enforcement and other actions taken thereunder, together with such recommendations for legislative and other action as he deems appropriate.

SECTION 12.

There are authorized to be appropriated to carry out this Act $125,000 for the period beginning July 1, 1976, and ending September 30, 1976; and for the fiscal year beginning October 1, 1976, and for each fiscal year thereafter there are authorized to be appropriated such sums, not to exceed $500,000, as may be necessary to carry out this Act.

APPENDIX 17:
THE FEDERAL ANIMAL WELFARE ACT
(7 U.S.C. §§2131 ET SEQ.)

§ 2131. TITLE AND FINDINGS

(a) This Act may be cited as the "Animal Welfare Act."

(b) The Congress finds that animals and activities which are regulated under this Act are either in interstate or foreign commerce or substantially affect such commerce or the free flow thereof, and that regulation of animals and activities a provided in this Act is necessary to prevent and eliminate burdens upon such commerce and to effectively regulate such commerce, in order:

(1) to insure that animals intended for use in research facilities or for exhibition purposes or for use as pets are provided humane care and treatment;

(2) to assure the humane treatment of animals during transportation in commerce; and

(3) to protect the owners of animals from the theft of their animals by preventing the sale or use of animals which have been stolen.

The Congress further finds that it is essential to regulate, as provided in this Act, the transportation, purchase, sale, housing, care, handling, and treatment of animals by carriers or by persons or organizations engaged in using them for research or experimental purposes or for exhibition purposes or holding them for sale as pets or for any such purpose or use. The congress further finds that:

(1) the use of animals is instrumental in certain research and education for advancing knowledge of cures and treatment for diseases and injuries which afflict both humans and animals;

(2) methods of testing that do not use animals are being and continue to be developed which are faster, less expensive, and more accurate than traditional animal experiments for some purposes and further opportunities exist for the development of these methods of testing;

(3) measures which eliminate or minimize the unnecessary duplication of experiments on animals can result in more productive use of Federal funds; and

(4) measures which help meet the public concern for laboratory animal care and treatment are important in assuring that research will continue to progress.

§ 2132. DEFINITIONS.

§ 2133. LICENSING OF DEALERS AND EXHIBITORS

The Secretary shall issue licenses to dealers and exhibitors upon application therefor in such form and manner as he may prescribe and upon payment of such fee established pursuant to 2153 of this title: Provided, That no such license shall be issued until the dealer or exhibitor shall have demonstrated that his facilities comply with the standards promulgated by the Secretary pursuant to section 2143 of this title: Provided, however, That any retail pet store or other person who derives less than a substantial portion of his income (as determined by the Secretary) from the breeding and raising of dogs or cats on his own premises and sells any such dog or cat to a dealer or research facility shall not be required to obtain a license as a dealer or exhibitor under this chapter. The Secretary is further authorized to license, as dealers or exhibitors, persons who do not qualify as dealers or exhibitors within the meaning of this chapter upon such persons' complying with the requirements specified above and agreeing, in writing, to comply with all the requirements of this chapter and the regulations promulgated by the Secretary hereunder.

§ 2134. VALID LICENSE FOR DEALERS AND EXHIBITORS REQUIRED

No dealer or exhibitor shall sell or offer to sell or transport or offer for transportation, in commerce, to any research facility or for exhibition or for use as a pet any animal, or buy, sell, offer to buy or sell, transport or offer for transportation, in commerce, to or from another dealer or exhibitor under this chapter any animal, unless and until such dealer or exhibitor shall have obtained a license from the Secretary and such license shall not have been suspended or revoked.

§ 2135. TIME PERIOD FOR DISPOSAL OF DOGS OR CATS BY DEALERS OR EXHIBITORS

No dealer or exhibitor shall sell or otherwise dispose of any dog or cat within a period of five business days after the acquisition of such animal or within such other period as may be specified by the Secretary: Provided, That operators of auction sales subject to section 2142 of this title shall not be required to comply with the provisions of this section.

§ 2136. REGISTRATION OF RESEARCH FACILITIES, HANDLERS, CARRIERS AND UNLICENSED EXHIBITORS

Every research facility, every intermediate handler, every carrier, and every exhibitor not licensed under section 2133 of this title shall register with the Secretary in accordance with such rules and regulations as he may prescribe.

§ 2137. PURCHASE OF DOGS OR CATS BY RESEARCH FACILITIES PROHIBITED EXCEPT FROM AUTHORIZED OPERATORS OF AUCTION SALES AND LICENSED DEALERS OR EXHIBITORS

It shall be unlawful for any research facility to purchase any dog or cat from any person except an operator of an auction sale subject to section 2142 of this title or a person holding a valid license as a dealer or exhibitor issued by the Secretary pursuant to this chapter unless such person is exempted from obtaining such license under section 2133 of this title.

§ 2138. PURCHASE OF DOGS OR CATS BY UNITED STATES GOVERNMENT FACILITIES PROHIBITED EXCEPT FROM AUTHORIZED OPERATORS OF AUCTION SALES AND LICENSED DEALERS OR EXHIBITORS

No department, agency, or instrumentality of the United States which uses animals for research or experimentation or exhibition shall purchase or otherwise acquire any dog or cat for such purposes from any person except an operator of an auction sale subject to section 2142 of this title or a person holding a valid license as a dealer or exhibitor issued by the Secretary pursuant to this chapter unless such person is exempted from obtaining such license under section 2133 of this title.

§ 2139. PRINCIPAL-AGENT RELATIONSHIP ESTABLISHED

When construing or enforcing the provisions of this chapter, the act, omission, or failure of any person acting for or employed by a research facility, a dealer, or an exhibitor or a person licensed as a dealer or an exhibitor pursuant to the second sentence of section 2133 of this title, or an operator of an auction sale subject to section 2142 of this title, or an intermediate handler, or a carrier, within the scope of his employment or office, shall be deemed the act, omission, or failure of such research facility, dealer, exhibitor, licensee, operator of an auction sale, intermediate handler, or carrier, as well as of such person.

§ 2140. RECORDKEEPING BY DEALERS, EXHIBITORS, RESEARCH FACILITIES, INTERMEDIATE HANDLERS, AND CARRIERS

Dealers and exhibitors shall make and retain for such reasonable period of time as the Secretary may prescribe, such records with respect to the purchase, sale, transportation, identification, and previous ownership of animals as the Secretary may prescribe. Research facilities shall make and retain such records only with respect to the purchase, sale, transportation, identification, and previous ownership of live dogs and cats. At the request of the Secretary, any regulatory agency of the Federal Government which requires records to be maintained by intermediate handlers and carriers with respect to the transportation, receiving, handling, and delivery of animals on forms prescribed by the agency, shall require there to be included in such forms, and intermediate handlers and carriers shall include in such forms, such information as the Secretary may require for the effective administration of this chapter. Such information shall be retained for such reasonable period of time as the Secretary may prescribe. If regulatory agencies of the Federal Government do not prescribe requirements for any such forms, intermediate handlers and carriers shall make and retain for such reasonable period as the Secretary may prescribe such records with respect to the transportation, receiving, handling, and delivery of animals as the Secretary may prescribe. Such records shall be made available at all reasonable times for inspection and copying by the Secretary.

§ 2141. MARKING AND IDENTIFICATION OF ANIMALS

All animals delivered for transportation, transported, purchased, or sold, in commerce, by a dealer or exhibitor shall be marked or identified at such time and in such humane manner as the Secretary may prescribe: Provided, That only live dogs and cats need be so marked or identified by a research facility.

§ 2142. HUMANE STANDARDS AND RECORDKEEPING REQUIREMENTS AT AUCTION SALES

The Secretary is authorized to promulgate humane standards and recordkeeping requirements governing the purchase, handling, or sale of animals, in commerce, by dealers, research facilities, and exhibitors at auction sales and by the operators of such auction sales. The Secretary is also authorized to require the licensing of operators of auction sales where any dogs or cats are sold, in commerce, under such conditions as he may prescribe, and upon payment of such fee as prescribed by the Secretary under 2153 of this title.

2143. STANDARDS AND CERTIFICATION PROCESS FOR HUMANE HANDLING, CARE, TREATMENT AND TRANSPORTATION OF ANIMALS

a. Promulgation of standards, rules, regulations, and orders; requirements; research facilities; State authority

1. The Secretary shall promulgate standards to govern the humane handling, care, treatment, and transportation of animals by dealers, research facilities, and exhibitors.

2. The standards described in paragraph (1) shall include minimum requirements—

A. For handling, housing, feeding, watering, sanitation, ventilation, shelter from extremes of weather and temperatures, adequate veterinary care, and separation by species where the Secretary finds necessary for humane handling, care, or treatment of animals; and

B. For exercise of dogs, as determined by an attending veterinarian in accordance with general standards promulgated by the Secretary, and for a physical environment adequate to promote the psychological well-being of primates.

3. In addition to the requirements under paragraph (2), the standards described in paragraph (1) shall, with respect to animals in research facilities, include requirements—

A. For animal care, treatment, and practices in experimental procedures to ensure that animal pain and distress are minimized, including adequate veterinary care with the appropriate use of anesthetic, analgesic, tranquilizing drugs, or euthanasia;

B. that the principal investigator considers alternatives to any procedure likely to produce pain to or distress in an experimental animal;

C. in any practice which could cause pain to animals—

i. that a doctor of veterinary medicine is consulted in the planning of such procedures;

ii. for the use of tranquilizers, analgesics, and anesthetics;

iii. for pre-surgical and post-surgical care by laboratory workers, in accordance with established veterinary medical and nursing procedures;

iv. against the use of paralytics without anesthesia; and

v. that the withholding of tranquilizers, anesthesia, analgesia, or euthanasia when scientifically necessary shall continue for only the necessary period of time;

D. that no animal is used in more than one major operative experiment from which it is allowed to recover except in cases of—

i. scientific necessity; or

ii. other special circumstances as determined by the Secretary; and

E. that exceptions to such standards may be made only when specified by research protocol and that any such exception shall be detailed and explained in a report outlined under paragraph (7) and filed with the Institutional Animal Committee.

4. The Secretary shall also promulgate standards to govern the transportation in commerce, and the handling, care, and treatment in connection therewith, by intermediate handlers, air carriers, or other carriers, of animals consigned by any dealer, research facility, exhibitor, operator of an auction sale, or other person, or any department, agency, or instrumentality of the United States or of any State or local government, for transportation in commerce. The Secretary shall have authority to promulgate such rules and regulations as he determines necessary to assure humane treatment of animals in the course of their transportation in commerce including requirements such as those with respect to containers, feed, water, rest, ventilation, temperature, and handling.

5. In promulgating and enforcing standards established pursuant to this section, the Secretary is authorized and directed to consult experts, including outside consultants where indicated.

6.A. Nothing in this chapter—

i. except as provided in paragraphs [FN1] (7) of this subsection, shall be construed as authorizing the Secretary to promulgate rules, regulations, or orders with regard to the design, outlines, or guidelines of actual research or experimentation by a research facility as determined by such research facility;

ii. except as provided [FN2] subparagraphs (A) and (C)(ii) through (v) of paragraph (3) and paragraph (7) of this subsection, shall be construed as authorizing the Secretary to promulgate rules, regulations, or orders with regard to the performance of actual research or experimentation by a research facility as determined by such research facility; and

iii. shall authorize the Secretary, during inspection, to interrupt the conduct of actual research or experimentation.

6.B. No rule, regulation, order, or part of this chapter shall be construed to require a research facility to disclose publicly or to the Institutional Animal Committee during its inspection, trade secrets or commercial or financial information which is privileged or confidential.

7.A. The Secretary shall require each research facility to show upon inspection, and to report at least annually, that the provisions of this chapter are being followed and that professionally acceptable standards governing the care, treatment, and use of animals are being followed by the research facility during actual research or experimentation.

7.B. In complying with subparagraph (A), such research facilities shall provide—

i. information on procedures likely to produce pain or distress in any animal and assurances demonstrating that the principal investigator considered alternatives to those procedures;

ii. assurances satisfactory to the Secretary that such facility is adhering to the standards described in this section; and

iii. an explanation for any deviation from the standards promulgated under this section.

b. Paragraph (1) shall not prohibit any State (or a political subdivision of such State) from promulgating standards in addition to those standards promulgated by the Secretary under paragraph (1).

c. Research facility Committee; establishment, membership, functions, etc.

1. The Secretary shall require that each research facility establish at least one Committee. Each Committee shall be appointed by the chief executive officer of each such research facility and shall be composed of not fewer than three members. Such members shall possess sufficient ability to assess animal care, treatment, and practices in experimental research as determined by the needs of the research facility and shall represent society's concerns regarding the welfare of ani-

mal subjects used at such facility. Of the members of the Committee—

A. at least one member shall be a doctor of veterinary medicine;

B. at least one member—

i. shall not be affiliated in any way with such facility other than as a member of the Committee;

ii. shall not be a member of the immediate family of a person who is affiliated with such facility; and

iii. is intended to provide representation for general community interests in the proper care and treatment of animals; and

C. in those cases where the Committee consists of more than three members, not more than three members shall be from the same administrative unit of such facility.

2. A quorum shall be required for all formal actions of the Committee, including inspections under paragraph (3).

3. The Committee shall inspect at least semiannually all animal study areas and animal facilities of such research facility and review as part of the inspection—

A. practices involving pain to animals, and

B. the condition of animals, to ensure compliance with the provisions of this chapter to minimize pain and distress to animals. Exceptions to the requirement of inspection of such study areas may be made by the Secretary if animals are studied in their natural environment and the study area is prohibitive to easy access.

4.A. The Committee shall file an inspection certification report of each inspection at the research facility. Such report shall—

i. be signed by a majority of the Committee members involved in the inspection;

ii. include reports of any violation of the standards promulgated, or assurances required, by the Secretary, including any deficient conditions of animal care or treatment, any deviations of research practices from originally approved proposals that adversely affect animal welfare, any notification to the facility regarding such conditions, and any corrections made thereafter;

iii. include any minority views of the Committee; and

iv. include any other information pertinent to the activities of the Committee.

4.B. Such report shall remain on file for at least three years at the research facility and shall be available for inspection by the Animal and Plant Health Inspection Service and any funding Federal agency.

4.C. In order to give the research facility an opportunity to correct any deficiencies or deviations discovered by reason of paragraph (3), the Committee shall notify the administrative representative of the research facility of any deficiencies or deviations from the provisions of this chapter. If, after notification and an opportunity for correction, such deficiencies or deviations remain uncorrected, the Committee shall notify (in writing) the Animal and Plant Health Inspection Service and the funding Federal agency of such deficiencies or deviations.

5. The inspection results shall be available to Department of Agriculture inspectors for review during inspections. Department of Agriculture inspectors shall forward any Committee inspection records which include reports of uncorrected deficiencies or deviations to the Animal and Plant Health Inspection Service and any funding Federal agency of the project with respect to which such uncorrected deficiencies and deviations occurred.

d. Federal research facilities; establishment, composition, and responsibilities of Federal Committee

In the case of Federal research facilities, a Federal Committee shall be established and shall have the same composition and responsibilities provided in subsection (b) of this section, except that the Federal Committee shall report deficiencies or deviations to the head of the Federal agency conducting the research rather than to the Animal and Plant Health Inspection Service. The head of the Federal agency conducting the research shall be responsible for—

1. all corrective action to be taken at the facility; and

2. the granting of all exceptions to inspection protocol.

e. Training of scientists, animal technicians, and other personnel involved with animal care and treatment at research facilities

Each research facility shall provide for the training of scientists, animal technicians, and other personnel involved with animal care and treatment in such facility as required by the Secretary. Such training shall include instruction on—

1. the humane practice of animal maintenance and experimentation;

2. research or testing methods that minimize or eliminate the use of animals or limit animal pain or distress;

3. utilization of the information service at the National Agricultural Library, established under subsection (e) of this section; and

4. methods whereby deficiencies in animal care and treatment should be reported.

f. Establishment of information service at National Agricultural Library; service functions

The Secretary shall establish an information service at the National Agricultural Library. Such service shall, in cooperation with the National Library of Medicine, provide information—

1. pertinent to employee training;

2. which could prevent unintended duplication of animal experimentation as determined by the needs of the research facility; and

3. on improved methods of animal experimentation, including methods which could—

A. reduce or replace animal use; and

B. minimize pain and distress to animals, such as anesthetic and analgesic procedures.

g. Suspension or revocation of Federal support for research projects; prerequisites; appeal procedure

In any case in which a Federal agency funding a research project determines that conditions of animal care, treatment, or practice in a particular project have not been in compliance with standards promulgated under this chapter, despite notification by the Secretary or such Federal agency to the research facility and an opportunity for correction, such agency shall suspend or revoke Federal support for the project. Any research facility losing Federal support as a result of actions taken under the preceding sentence shall have the right of appeal as provided in sections 701 through 706 of Title 5.

h. Veterinary certificate; contents; exceptions

No dogs or cats, or additional kinds or classes of animals designated by regulation of the Secretary, shall be delivered by any dealer, research facility, exhibitor, operator of an auction sale, or department, agency, or instrumentality of the United States or of any State or local government, to any intermediate handler or carrier for transportation in commerce, or received by any such handler or carrier for such transportation from any such person, department, agency, or instrumentality, unless the animal is accompanied by a certificate issued by a veterinarian licensed to practice veterinary medicine, certifying that he inspected the animal on a specified date, which shall not be more than ten days before such delivery, and, when so inspected, the animal appeared free of any infectious disease or physical abnormality which would endanger the animal or animals or other animals or endanger public health: Provided, however, That the Secretary may by regulation provide exceptions to this certification requirement, under such conditions as he may prescribe in the regulations, for animals shipped to research facilities for purposes of research, testing or experimentation requiring animals not eligible for such certification. Such certificates received by the intermediate handlers and the carriers shall be retained by them, as provided by regulations of the Secretary, in accordance with section 2140 of this title.

i. Age of animals delivered to registered research facilities; power of Secretary to designate additional classes of animals and age limits

No dogs or cats, or additional kinds or classes of animals designated by regulation of the Secretary, shall be delivered by any person to any intermediate handler or carrier for transportation in commerce except to registered research facilities if they are less than such age as the Secretary may by regulation prescribe. The Secretary shall designate additional kinds and classes of animals and may prescribe different ages for particular kinds or classes of dogs, cats, or designated animals, for the purposes of this section, when he determines that such action is necessary or adequate to assure their humane treatment in connection with their transportation in commerce.

j. Prohibition of C.O.D. arrangements for transportation of animals in commerce; exceptions

No intermediate handler or carrier involved in the transportation of any animal in commerce shall participate in any arrangement or engage in any practice under which the cost of such animal or the cost of the transportation of such animal is to be paid and collected upon delivery of the animal to the consignee, unless the consignor guarantees in writing the payment of transportation charges for any animal not claimed within a period of 48 hours after notice to the consignee of arrival of the animal, including, where necessary, both the return transportation charges and an amount sufficient to reimburse the carrier for all out-of-pocket expenses incurred for the care, feeding, and storage of such animals.

§ 2144. HUMANE STANDARDS FOR ANIMALS BY UNITED STATES GOVERNMENT FACILITIES

Any department, agency, or instrumentality of the United States having laboratory animal facilities shall comply with the standards and other requirements promulgated by the Secretary for a research facility under sections 2143(a), (f), (g), and (h) of this title. Any department, agency, or instrumentality of the United States exhibiting animals shall comply with the standards promulgated by the Secretary under sections 2143(a), (f), (g), and (h) of this title.

§ 2145. CONSULTATION AND COOPERATION WITH FEDERAL, STATE, AND LOCAL GOVERNMENTAL BODIES BY SECRETARY OF AGRICULTURE

a. The Secretary shall consult and cooperate with other Federal departments, agencies, or instrumentalities concerned with the welfare of animals used for research, experimentation or exhibition, or administration of statutes regulating the transportation in commerce or handling in connection therewith of any animals when establishing standards pursuant to section 2143 of this title and in carrying out the purposes of this chapter. The Secretary shall consult with the Secretary of Health and Human Services prior to issuance of regulations. Before promulgating any standard governing the air transportation and handling in connection therewith, of animals, the Secretary shall consult with the Secretary of Transportation who shall have the authority to disapprove any such standard if he notifies the Secretary, within 30 days after such consultation, that changes in its provisions are necessary in the interest of flight safety. The Surface Transportation Board, the Secretary of Transportation, and the Federal Maritime Commission, to the extent of their respective lawful authorities, shall take such action as is appropriate to implement any standard established by the Secretary with respect to a person subject to regulation by it.

b. The Secretary is authorized to cooperate with the officials of the

various States or political subdivisions thereof in carrying out the purposes of this chapter and of any State, local, or municipal legislation or ordinance on the same subject.

§ 2146. ADMINISTRATION AND ENFORCEMENT BY SECRETARY

a. Investigations and inspections

The Secretary shall make such investigations or inspections as he deems necessary to determine whether any dealer, exhibitor, intermediate handler, carrier, research facility, or operator of an auction sale subject to section 2142 of this title, has violated or is violating any provision of this chapter or any regulation or standard issued thereunder, and for such purposes, the Secretary shall, at all reasonable times, have access to the places of business and the facilities, animals, and those records required to be kept pursuant to section 2140 of this title of any such dealer, exhibitor, intermediate handler, carrier, research facility, or operator of an auction sale. The Secretary shall inspect each research facility at least once each year and, in the case of deficiencies or deviations from the standards promulgated under this chapter, shall conduct such follow-up inspections as may be necessary until all deficiencies or deviations from such standards are corrected. The Secretary shall promulgate such rules and regulations as he deems necessary to permit inspectors to confiscate or destroy in a humane manner any animal found to be suffering as a result of a failure to comply with any provision of this chapter or any regulation or standard issued thereunder if (1) such animal is held by a dealer, (2) such animal is held by an exhibitor, (3) such animal is held by a research facility and is no longer required by such research facility to carry out the research, test, or experiment for which such animal has been utilized, (4) such animal is held by an operator of an auction sale, or (5) such animal is held by an intermediate handler or a carrier.

b. Penalties for interfering with official duties

Any person who forcibly assaults, resists, opposes, impedes, intimidates, or interferes with any person while engaged in or on account of the performance of his official duties under this chapter shall be fined not more than $5,000, or imprisoned not more than three years, or both. Whoever, in the commission of such acts, uses a deadly or dangerous weapon shall be fined not more than $10,000, or imprisoned not more than ten years, or both. Whoever kills any person while engaged in or on account of the performance of his official duties under this chapter shall be punished as provided under sections 1111 and 1114 of Title 18.

c. Procedures

For the efficient administration and enforcement of this chapter and the regulations and standards promulgated under this chapter, the provisions (including penalties) of sections 46, 48, 49 and 50 of Title 15 (except paragraph (c) through (h) of section 46 and the last paragraph of section 49 of Title 15), and the provisions of Title II of the Organized Crime Control Act of 1970, are made applicable to the jurisdiction, powers, and duties of the Secretary in administering and enforcing the provisions of this chapter and to any person, firm, or corporation with respect to whom such authority is exercised. The Secretary may prosecute any inquiry necessary to his duties under this chapter in any part of the United States, including any territory, or possession thereof, the District of Columbia, or the Commonwealth of Puerto Rico. The powers conferred by said sections 49 and 50 of Title 15 on the district courts of the United States may be exercised for the purposes of this chapter by any district court of the United States. The United States district courts, the District Court of Guam, the District Court of the Virgin Islands, the highest court of American Samoa, and the United States courts of the other territories, are vested with jurisdiction specifically to enforce, and to prevent and restrain violations of this chapter, and shall have jurisdiction in all other kinds of cases arising under this chapter, except as provided in section 2149(c) of this title.

§ 2147. INSPECTION BY LEGALLY CONSTITUTED LAW ENFORCEMENT AGENCIES

The Secretary shall promulgate rules and regulations requiring dealers, exhibitors, research facilities, and operators of auction sales subject to section 2142 of this title to permit inspection of their animals and records at reasonable hours upon request by legally constituted law enforcement agencies in search of lost animals.

§ 2148. REPEALED. PUB. L. 91-579, 19, DEC. 24, 1970, 84 STAT. 1564

§ 2149. VIOLATIONS BY LICENSEES

a. Temporary license suspension; notice and hearing; revocation

If the Secretary has reason to believe that any person licensed as a dealer, exhibitor, or operator of an auction sale subject to section 2142 of this title, has violated or is violating any provision of this chapter, or any of the rules or regulations or standards promulgated by the Secretary hereunder, he may suspend such person's license temporarily, but not to exceed 21 days, and after notice and opportunity for hearing, may suspend for such additional period as he may specify, or revoke such license, if such violation is determined to have occurred.

b. Civil penalties for violation of any section, etc.; separate offenses; notice and hearing; appeal; considerations in assessing penalty; compromise of penalty; civil action by Attorney General for failure to pay penalty; district court jurisdiction; failure to obey cease and desist order

Any dealer, exhibitor, research facility, intermediate handler, carrier, or operator of an auction sale subject to section 2142 of this title, that violates any provision of this chapter, or any rule, regulation, or standard promulgated by the Secretary thereunder, may be assessed a civil penalty by the Secretary of not more than $2,500 for each such violation, and the Secretary may also make an order that such person shall cease and desist from continuing such violation. Each violation and each day during which a violation continues shall be a separate offense. No penalty shall be assessed or cease and desist order issued unless such person is given notice and opportunity for a hearing with respect to the alleged violation, and the order of the Secretary assessing a penalty and making a cease and desist order shall be final and conclusive unless the affected person files an appeal from the Secretary's order with the appropriate United States Court of Appeals. The Secretary shall give due consideration to the appropriateness of the penalty with respect to the size of the business of the person involved, the gravity of the violation, the person's good faith, and the history of previous violations. Any such civil penalty may be compromised by the Secretary. Upon any failure to pay the penalty assessed by a final order under this section, the Secretary shall request the Attorney General to a civil action in a district court of the United States or other United States court for any district in which such person is found or resides or transacts business, to collect the penalty, and such court shall have jurisdiction to hear and decide any such action. Any person who knowingly fails to obey a cease and desist order made by the Secretary under this section shall be subject to a civil penalty of $1,500 for each offense, and each day during which such failure continues shall be deemed a separate offense.

c. Appeal of final order by aggrieved person; limitations; exclusive jurisdiction of United States Courts of Appeals

Any dealer, exhibitor, research facility, intermediate handler, carrier, or operator of an auction sale subject to section 2142 of this title, aggrieved by a final order of the Secretary issued pursuant to this section may, within 60 days after entry of such an order, seek review of such order in the appropriate United States Court of Appeals in accordance with the provisions of sections 2341, 2343 through 2350 of Title 28, and such court shall have exclusive jurisdiction to enjoin, set aside, suspend (in whole or in part), or to determine the validity of the Secretary's order.

d. Criminal penalties for violation; initial prosecution brought before United States magistrate judges; conduct of prosecution by attorneys of United States Department of Agriculture

Any dealer, exhibitor, or operator of an auction sale subject to section 2142 of this title, who knowingly violates any provision of this chapter shall, on conviction thereof, be subject to imprisonment for not more than 1 year, or a fine of not more than $2,500, or both. Prosecution of such violations shall, to the maximum extent practicable, be brought before United States magistrates as provided in section 636 of Title 28, and sections 3401 and 3402 of Title 18, and, with the consent of the Attorney General, may be conducted, at both trial and upon appeal to district court, by attorneys of the United States Department of Agriculture.

§ 2150. REPEALED. PUB.L. 94-279, 14, APR. 22, 1976, 90 STAT. 421

§ 2151. RULES AND REGULATIONS

The Secretary is authorized to promulgate such rules, regulations, and orders as he may deem necessary in order to effectuate the purposes of this chapter.

§ 2152. SEPARABILITY

If any provision of this chapter or the application of any such provision to any person or circumstances shall be held invalid, the remainder of this chapter and the application of any such provision to persons or circumstances other than those as to which it is held invalid shall not be affected thereby.

§ 2153. FEES AND AUTHORIZATION OF APPROPRIATIONS

The Secretary shall charge, assess, and cause to be collected reasonable fees for licenses issued. Such fees shall be adjusted on an equitable basis taking into consideration the type and nature of the operations to be licensed and shall be deposited and covered into the Treasury as miscellaneous receipts. There are hereby authorized to be appropriated such funds as Congress may from time to time provide: Provided, That there is authorized to be appropriated to the Secretary of Agriculture for enforcement by the Department of Agriculture of the provisions of section 2156 of this title an amount not to exceed $100,000 for the transition quarter ending September 30, 1976, and not to exceed $400,000 for each fiscal year thereafter.

§ 2154. EFFECTIVE DATES

The regulations referred to in sections 2140 and 2143 of this title shall be prescribed by the Secretary as soon as reasonable but not later than six months from August 24, 1966. Additions and amendments thereto be prescribed from time to time as may be necessary or advisable. Compliance by dealers with the provisions of this chapter and such regulations shall commence ninety days after the promulgation of such regulations. Compliance by research facilities with the provisions of this chapter and such regulations shall commence six months after the promulgation of such regulations, except that the Secretary may grant extensions of time to research facilities which do not comply with the prescribed by the Secretary pursuant to section 2143 of this title provided that the Secretary determines that there is evidence that the research facilities will meet such standards within a reasonable time. Notwithstanding the other provisions of this section, compliance by intermediate handlers, and carriers, and other persons with those provisions of this chapter, as amended by the Animal Welfare Act Amendments of 1976, and those regulations promulgated thereunder, which relate to actions of intermediate handlers and carriers, shall commence 90 days after promulgation of regulations under section 2143 of this title, as amended, with respect to intermediate handlers and carriers, and such regulations shall be promulgated no later than 9 months after April 22, 1976; and compliance by dealers, exhibitors, operators of auction sales, and research facilities with other provisions of this chapter, as so amended, and the regulations thereunder, shall commence upon the expiration of 90 days after April 22, 1976: Provided, however, That compliance by all persons with subsections (b), (c), and (d) of section 2143 and with section 2156 of this title, as so amended, shall commence upon the expiration of said ninety-day period. In all other respects, said amendments shall become effective upon April 22, 1976.

§ 2155. ANNUAL REPORT TO THE PRESIDENT OF THE SENATE AND THE SPEAKER OF THE HOUSE OF REPRESENTATIVES

Not later than March of each year, the Secretary shall submit to the President of the Senate and the Speaker of the House of Representatives a comprehensive and detailed written report with respect to—

1. the identification of all research facilities, exhibitors, and other persons and establishments licensed by the Secretary under section 2133 and section 2142 of this title;

2. the nature and place of all investigations and inspections conducted by the Secretary under section 2146 of this title, and all reports received by the Secretary under section 2143 of this title;

3. recommendations for legislation to improve the administration of this chapter or any provisions thereof;

4. recommendations and conclusions concerning the aircraft environment as it relates to the carriage of live animals in air transportation; and

5. the information and recommendations described in section 1830 of Title 15.

This report as well as any supporting documents, data, or findings shall not be released to any other persons, non-Federal agencies, or organizations unless and until it has been made public by an appropriate committee of the Senate or the House of Representatives.

§ 2156. ANIMAL FIGHTING VENTURE PROHIBITION

a. Sponsoring or exhibiting animal in any fighting venture

It shall be unlawful for any person to knowingly sponsor or exhibit an animal in any animal fighting venture to which any animal was moved in interstate or foreign commerce.

b. Buying, selling, delivering, or transporting animals for participation in animal fighting venture

It shall be unlawful for any person to knowingly sell, buy, transport, or deliver to another person or receive from another person for purposes of transportation, in interstate or foreign commerce, any dog or other animal for purposes of having the dog or other animal participate in an animal fighting venture.

c. Use of Postal Service or other interstate instrumentality for promoting or furthering animal fighting venture

It shall be unlawful for any person to knowingly use the mail service of the United States Postal Service or any interstate instrumentality for purposes of promoting or in any other manner furthering an animal fighting venture except as performed outside the limits of the States of the United States.

d. Violation of State law

Notwithstanding the provisions of subsections (a), (b), or (c) of this section, the activities prohibited by such subsections shall be unlawful with respect to fighting ventures involving live birds only if the fight is to take place in a State where it would be in violation of the laws thereof.

e. Penalties

Any person who violates subsection (a), (b), or (c) of this section shall be fined not more than $5,000 or imprisoned for not more than 1 year, or both, for each such violation.

f. Investigation of violations by Secretary; assistance by other Federal agencies; issuance of search warrant; forfeiture; costs recoverable in forfeiture or civil action

The Secretary or any other person authorized by him shall make such investigations as the Secretary deems necessary to determine whether any person has violated or is violating any provision of this section, and the Secretary may obtain the assistance of the Federal Bureau of Investigation, the Department of the Treasury, or other law enforcement agencies of the United States, and State and local governmental agencies, in the conduct of such investigations, under cooperative agreements with such agencies. A warrant to search for and seize any animal which there is probable cause to believe was involved in any violation of this section may be issued by any judge of the United States or of a State court of record or by a United States magistrate within the district wherein the animal sought is located. Any United States marshal or any person authorized under this section to conduct investigations may apply for and execute any such warrant, and any animal seized under such a warrant shall be held by the United States marshal or other authorized person pending disposition thereof by the court in accordance with this subsection. Necessary care including veterinary treatment shall be provided while the animals are so held in custody. Any animal involved in any violation of this section shall be liable to be proceeded against and forfeited to the United States at any time on complaint filed in any United States district court or other court of the United States for any jurisdiction in which the animal is found and upon a judgment of forfeiture shall be disposed of by sale for lawful purposes or by other humane means, as the court may direct. Costs incurred by the United States for care of animals seized and forfeited under this section shall be recoverable from the owner of the animals if he appears in such forfeiture proceeding or in a separate civil action brought in the jurisdiction in which the owner is found, resides, or transacts business.

g. Definitions

For purposes of this section—

1. the term "animal fighting venture" means any event which involves a fight between at least two animals and is conducted for purposes of sport, wagering, or entertainment except that the term "animal fighting venture" shall not be deemed to include any activity the primary purpose of which involves the use of one or more animals in hunting another animal or animals, such as waterfowl, bird, raccoon, or fox hunting;

2. the term "interstate or foreign commerce" means—

A. any movement between any place in a State to any place in another State or between places in the same State through another State; or

B. any movement from a foreign country into any State;

3. the term "interstate instrumentality" means telegraph, telephone, radio, or television operating in interstate or foreign commerce;

4. the term "State" means any State of the United States, the District of Columbia, the Commonwealth of Puerto Rico, and any territory or possession of the United States;

5. the term "animal" means any live bird, or any live dog or other mammal, except man; and

6. the conduct by any person of any activity prohibited by this section shall not render such person subject to the other sections of this chapter as a dealer, exhibitor, or otherwise.

h. Conflict with State law

The provisions of this chapter shall not supersede or otherwise invalidate any such State, local, or municipal legislation or ordinance relating to animal fighting ventures except in case of a direct and irreconcilable conflict between any requirements thereunder and this chapter or any rule, regulation, or standard hereunder.

§ 2157. RELEASE OF TRADE SECRETS

a. Release of confidential information prohibited

It shall be unlawful for any member of an Institutional Animal Committee to release any confidential information of the research facility including any information that concerns or relates to—

1. the trade secrets, processes, operations, style of work, or apparatus; or

2. the identity, confidential statistical data, amount or source of any income, profits, losses, or expenditures, of the research facility.

b. Wrongful use of confidential information prohibited

It shall be unlawful for any member of such Committee—

1. to use or attempt to use to his advantages; or

2. to revel to any other person, any information which is entitled to protection as confidential information under subsection (a) of this section.

c. Penalties

A violation of subsection (a) or (b) of this section is punishable by—

1. removal from such Committee; and

2. A. a fine of not more than $1,000 and imprisonment of not more than one year; or

2. B. if such violation is willful, a fine of not more than $10,000 and imprisonment of not more than three years.

d. Recovery of damages by injured person; costs; attorney's fee

Any person, including any research facility, injured in its business or property by reason of a violation of this section may recover all actual and consequential damages sustained by such person and the cost of the suit including a reasonable attorney's fee.

e. Other rights and remedies

Nothing in this section shall be construed to affect any other rights of a person injured in its business or property by reason of a violation of this section. Subsection (d) of this section shall not be construed to the exercise of any such rights arising out of or relating to a violation of subsections (a) and (b) of this section.

§ 2158. PROTECTION OF PETS

a. Holding period

1. Requirement

In the case of each dog or cat acquired by an entity described in paragraph (2), such entity shall hold and care for such dog or cat for a period of not less than five days to enable such dog or cat to be recovered by its original owner or adopted by other individuals before such entity sells such dog or cat to a dealer.

2. Entities described

An entity subject to paragraph (1) is—

> A. each State, county, or city owned and operated pound or shelter;
>
> B. each private entity established for the purpose of caring for animals, such as a humane society, or other organization that is under contract with a State, county, or city that operates as a pound or shelter and that releases animals on a voluntary basis; and
>
> C. each research facility licensed by the Department of Agriculture.

b. Certification

1. In general

> A dealer may not sell, provide, or make available to any individual or entity a random source dog or cat unless such dealer provides the recipient with a valid certification that meets the requirements of paragraph (2) and indicates compliance with subsection (a) of this section.

2. Requirements

A valid certification shall contain—

A. the name, address, and Department of Agriculture license or registration number (if such number exists) of the dealer;

Bathe name, address, Department of Agriculture license or registration number (if such number exists), and the signature of the recipient of the dog or cat;

CIA description of the dog or cat being provided that shall include—

i. the species and breed or type of such;

ii. the sex of such;

iii. the date of birth (if known) of such;

iv. the color and any distinctive marking of such; and

v. any other information that the Secretary by regulation shall determine to be appropriate;

D. the name and address of the person, pound, or shelter from which the dog or cat was purchased or otherwise acquired by the dealer, and an assurance that such person, pound, or shelter was notified that such dog or cat may be used for research or educational purposes;

E. the date of the purchase or acquisition referred to in subparagraph (D);

F. a statement by the pound or shelter (if the dealer acquired the dog or cat from such) that it satisfied the requirements of subsection (a) of this section; and

G. any other information that the Secretary of Agriculture by regulation shall determine appropriate.

3. Records

The original certification required under paragraph (1) shall accompany the shipment of a dog or cat to be sold, provided, or otherwise made available by the dealer, and shall be kept and maintained by the research facility for a period of at least one year for enforcement purposes. The dealer shall retain one copy of the certification provided under this paragraph for a period of at least one year for enforcement

4. Transfers

In instances where one research facility transfers animals to another research facility a copy of the certificate must accompany such transfer.

5. Modification

Certification requirements may be modified to reflect technological advances in identification techniques, such as microchip technology, if the Secretary determines that adequate information such as described in this section, will be collected, transferred, and maintained through technology.

c. Enforcement

1. In general

Dealers who fail to act according to the requirements of this section or who include false information in the certification required under subsection (b) of this section, shall be subject to the penalties provided for under section 2149 of this title.

2. Subsequent violations

Any dealer who violates this section more than one time shall be subject to a fine of $5,000 per dog or cat acquired or sold in violation of this section.

3. Permanent revocations

Any dealer who violates this section three or more times shall have such dealers license permanently revoked.

d. Regulation

Not later than 180 days after November 28, 1990, the Secretary shall promulgate regulations to carry out this section.

§ 2159. AUTHORITY TO APPLY FOR INJUNCTIONS

a. Request

Whenever the Secretary has reason to believe that any dealer, carrier, exhibitor, or intermediate handler is dealing in stolen animals, or is placing the health of any animal in serious danger in violation of this chapter or the regulations or standards promulgated thereunder, the Secretary shall notify the Attorney General, who may apply to the United district court in which such dealer, carrier, exhibitor, or intermediate handler resides or conducts business for a temporary restraining order or injunction to prevent any such person from operating in violation of this chapter or the regulations and standards prescribed under this chapter.

b. Issuance

The court shall, upon a proper showing, issue a temporary restraining order or injunction under subsection (a) of this section without bond. Such injunction or order shall remain in effect until a complaint pursuant to section 2149 of this title is issued and dismissed by the Secretary or until an order to cease and desist made thereon by the Secretary has become final and effective or is set aside on appellate review. Attorneys of the Department of Agriculture may, with the approval of the Attorney General, appear in the United States district court representing the Secretary in any action brought under this section.

APPENDIX 18:
NATIONAL ANIMAL RIGHTS ORGANIZATIONS

Name	Address	Phone	Fax	Email	URL	Mission
Action for Animals	SAO 176 HUB 207, Box 352238 Seattle, WA 98195	206-227-5752	n/a	afa@afa-on-line.org	http://www.afa-online.org	AFA strives to end animal suffering through educational outreach, demonstrations, and local media involvement

Name	Address	Phone	Fax	Email	URL	Mission
Action for Animals Network	PO Box 9039, Alexandria, VA 22304	703-461-3283	703-461-3283	anmlntwk@erols.com	http://www.enviroweb.org/aan	AAN focuses mainly on animals who suffer in the meat and dairy industries and in circuses
All For Animals	1324 State Street, #J109 Santa Barbara, CA 93101	805-682-3160	805-569-9810	info@allforanimals.com	http://www.allforanimals.com	pro-animal organization dedicated to informing and educating people about cruelty-free living and the rights of all animals
Alliance for Animals	122 State Street, #406, Madison, 53703	608-257-6333	608-257-6400	alliance@allanimals.org	http://www.allanimals.org	devoted to increasing public awareness of animal abuse and promoting the humane treatment of all animals

Name	Address	Phone	Fax	Email	URL	Mission
Alliance for the Wild Rockies	PO Box 8731, Missoula, MO 59807	406-721-5420	406-721-9917	awr@wildrockies alliance.org	http://www.wildro ckiesalliance.org	formed to save the Northern Rockies Bioregion from habitat destruction
American Anti-Vivisection Society	801 Old York Rd, Suite 204, Jenkintown, PA 19046-1685	215-887-0816	215-887-2088	aavsonline@aol. com	http://www.aavs. org	dedicated to ending the use of animals in research, testing and education
Animal Defense League–New York City	PO Box 20878, New York, 10009	917-724-8126	n/a	NYC_ADL@big-foot.com	http://mem-bers.aol.com/adln ycli/home.htm	nationally active, grassroots, animal liberation and defense organization
Animal Haven	35-22 Prince Street, Flushing, NY 11354	718-886-3683	n/a	animalhaveninc@ aol.com	http://www.anima lhavenshelter.org	a no-kill shelter for abandoned animals in New York City

Name	Address	Phone	Fax	Email	URL	Mission
American Humane Association	63 Inverness Drive East, Englewood, CO 80112-5117	303-792-9900	303-792-5333	animal@ americanhumane. org	http://www.amerh umane.org	mission is to prevent cruelty, abuse, neglect and exploitation of animals
American Humane Association Film and TV Unit	15366 Dickens Street, Sylmar, 91403	818-501—0123	818-501-8725	geebrr@aol.com	http://www.AHAFi lm.org	monitors the care and treatment of animals used in filmed media
Animallaw.com	NAVS 53 West Jackson Street, 15th floor, Chicago, IL 60604	312-427-6065	n/a	g_a_wachtel@ya-hoo.com	http://www.anima llaw.com	a comprehensive online resource which disseminates legal and legislative information as it pertains to animal issues

Name	Address	Phone	Fax	Email	URL	Mission
Animal Legal Defense Fund	127 Fourth Street, Petaluma, CA 94952	707-769-7771	707-769-0785	info@aldf.org	http://www.aldf.org	leading animal rights law organization working nationally to defend animals from abuse and exploitation
Animal Liberation of Texas	PO Box 820872, Dallas, TX 75382	972-664-6760	214-342-8957	ALTdallas@aol.com	http://www.animaliberation.com	ALT's mission is to stop the torture and suffering of animals
Animal Lifeline	POBox 981, Waterford, NJ 08089	n/a	n/a	squash1098@earthlink.net	http://www.angelfire.com/nj2/animalifeline	dedicated to finding loving homes for pets
Animal Place	3448 Laguna Creek Trail, Vacaville, CA 95688-9724	707-449-4814	707-449-8775	AnimalPlace@aol.com	http://www.enviroweb.org/animal_place	a nonprofit sanctuary for abused and discarded farm animals

Name	Address	Phone	Fax	Email	URL	Mission
Animal Protection Institute	Sacramento, CA 95820	916-731-5521	916-731-4467	LawrenceCarter-Long@api4animals.org	http://www.api4animals.org	dedicated to informing, educating, and advocating the humane treatment of all animals
Animal Refuge Foundation	3377 Spalding Rd, Sherman, TX 75092	903-564-7056	n/a	arf@arfhouse.com	http://www.arfhouse.com	a no-kill "care-for-life" canine sanctuary which provides refuge and care for unwanted, abused and/or physically challenged canines
Animal Rescue Foundation	251 Underwood Road, PO Box 1032, Milledgeville, GA 31061	912-454-1273	n/a	arf@accucomm.net	http://www.animalrescuefoundation.org	mission includes finding responsible permanent homes as family pets for abandoned animals

Name	Address	Phone	Fax	Email	URL	Mission
Animal Rights Advocates of Western New York	PO Box 475, Buffalo, NY 14226	716-648-6423	716-648-6423	ARAofWNY@aol.com	http://www.geocities.com/arawny	dedicated to the elimination of animal abuse and exploitation
Animal Rights Coalition	3867 Winter Berry Road, Jacksonville, FL 32210	904-781-2620	n/a	emcue@juno.com	http://www.arc-.org	mission is to educate the public on animal issues
Animal Rescue and Adoption Society	2390 S. Delaware St., Denver, CO 80223	303-744-6076	303-744-6075	mehughes@du.edu	http://arascolorado.tripod.com	a no-kill non-profit cat shelter
Animal Shelter	PO Box 770707, Winter Garden, FL 34777-0707	407-877-PETS	407-877-3292	pets@animalshelter.org	http://www.animalshelter.org	a non-profit organization whose mission is to help care for homeless pets
Animal Welfare Institute	PO Box 3650, Washington, DC 20007	202-537-2332	202-538-9478	awi@awionline.org	http://www.awionline.org	mission is to reduce the pain and fear inflicted on animals by humans

Name	Address	Phone	Fax	Email	URL	Mission
Animal Welfare League	10305 Southwest Highway, Chicago Ridge, IL 60415	(708)636-8586	708)636-9488	awl@wans.net.	http://www.anima lwelfareleague. com	mission is to prevent cruelty to animals and provide quality homes for animals through an adoption program
Ark-Haven Animal Sanctuary	PO Box 1559, McMinnville, OR 97128	503-843-1196	n/a	bj@ark-haven.org	http://www.ark-ha ven.org	a no-kill sanctuary dedicated to the rescue, rehabilitation and long term care of abused and neglected dogs, cats, and farm animals
Association of Veterinarians for Animal Rights	PO Box 208, Davis, CA 95617-0208	530-759-8106	530-759-8116	AVAR@igc.org	http://www.avar. org	mission is to reform the way society treats all nonhumans

Name	Address	Phone	Fax	Email	URL	Mission
Badlands Animal League	4661-105 Ave. SW, Dickinson, ND 58601	n/a	n/a	bal@pop.ctctel. com	http://bdlsanlg. webjump.com	mission is to reduce the animal population through spay-neuter programs and the construction of a no-kill animal shelter
Best Friends Animal Sanctuary	5001 Angel Canyon Drive, Kanab, UT 84741-5001	435-644-2001	435-644-2078	info@bestfriends. org	http://www.bestfri ends.org/in-dex.htm	the nation's largest sanctuary for abused and abandoned cats and dogs and other animals
Bide-A-Wee	410 east 38th Street, New York, NY 10016	212-532-6395	n/a	bawpr@aol.com	http://www.bidea wee.org	a non-profit animal shelter and humane society whose mission is to match responsible people with homeless pets

Name	Address	Phone	Fax	Email	URL	Mission
Cats Haven	PO Box 30206, Indianapolis, IN 46230	n/a	n/a	n/a	http://www.indy.net/~catshavn	a pro-life, no-kill shelter for cats and kittens who are in transition
Center For Captive Chimpanzee Care	PO Box 3746, Boynton Beach, FL 33424	561-963-8050	561-641-3246	info@savethechimps.org	http://www.savethechimps.org	mission is to create a sanctuary for the permanent, lifetime care for chimpanzees retired from research laboratories or who have been abandoned by owners no longer able to provide adequate care
Coalition for Animals	PO Box 611, Somerville, NJ 08876	908-281-0086	n/a	njcfa@worldnet.att.net	http://home.att.net/~njcfa	mission is to institute changes that will end animal exploitation and abuse

Name	Address	Phone	Fax	Email	URL	Mission
Companion Animal Protection Society	PMB 143, 2100 West Drake Road, Fort Collins, CO 80526	970-223-8300	970-223-8330	caps2@mindspring.com	http://www.cas-web.org	mission is ending the suffering of pet shop and puppy mill dogs
Cornell Coalition for Animal Defense	PO Box 39, Willard Straight Hall, Cornell University, Ithaca, NY 14853	607-279-6717	n/a	ccad@cornell.edu	http://www.rso. cornell.edu/ccad	an active group of animal liberation activists on the Cornell University campus
Defenders Of Animals	PO Box 5634, Weybosset Hill Station, Providence, RI 02903-0634	401-738-3710	n/a	dennis@defendersof animals.org	http://www.defend ersofanimals.org	mission is to provide assistance to sick, injured and homeless animals
Doris Day Animal League	227 Massachusetts Ave. NE, Suite 100, Washington, DC 20002	202-546-1761	n/a	info@ddal.org	http://www.ddal. org	dedicated to animal protection issues
Dream Catcher Farm Horse Sanctuary	Rocky Mount, VA 24151	540-489-3805	n/a	equine@horsesan ctuary.com	http://www.horses anctuary.com	horse sanctuary for abused, neglected and elderly equine

Name	Address	Phone	Fax	Email	URL	Mission
Elephant Sanctuary	PO Box 393, Hohenwald, TN 38462	931-796-6500	931-796-4810	elephant@elephants.com	http://www.elephants.com	the nation's first natural habitat refuge developed specifically for endangered Asian elephants
Endangered Species Coalition	1101 14th Street NW, Suite 1200, Washington, DC 20005	202)682-9400	202)682-1331	esc@stopextinction.org	http://www.stopextinction.org	the coalition supports stronger protections for the nation's imperiled wildlife
FARM—Farm Animal Reform Movement	PO Box 30654, Bethesda, MD 20824	301-530-1737	n/a	farm@farm.org	http://www.farm.org	a national, tax-exempt, educational organization advocating a plant-based diet and rights for farmed animals

Name	Address	Phone	Fax	Email	URL	Mission
Felines, Inc	PO Box 60616, Chicago, IL 60660	(773)465-4132	(773)465-6454	felinesinc@aol.com	http://www.felinesinc.org	mission is to care for and rehabilitate abandoned, abused and injured cats and kittens
Friends of Animals	777 Post Road, Darien, CT 06820	203-656-1522	n/a	icontact@friendsofanimals.org	http://www.friendsofanimals.org	a non-profit organization working to protect animals from cruelty and abuse
Green Acres Sanctuary	2867 Copper Kettle Hwy., Rockwood, PA 15557	814-926-4902	814-926-4902	info@greenacressanctuary.com	http://greenacressanctuary.com	a non-profit society for the prevention of cruelty to animals

Name	Address	Phone	Fax	Email	URL	Mission
Green Mountain Animal Defenders	PO Box 4577, Burlington, VT 05406	802-878-2230	n/a	SMacNair@gmad.net	http://gmad.net	a non-profit humane organization dedicated to finding loving, responsible homes for retired racing greyhounds
Greyhound Protection League	PO Box 669, Penn Valley, CA 95946	800-G-HOUNDS, 800-446-8637	n/a	greyhounds_org@bigfoot.com	http://www.greyhounds.org	a non-profit humane organization dedicated to protecting greyhounds from the exploitation and abuses inherent in the greyhound racing industry
Habitat for Horses, Inc.	PO Box 213, Hitchcock, 77563	409-935-0277	409-935-0424	admin@habitatforhorses.org	http://www.habitatforhorses.org	a sanctuary for retired horses from across the nation

Name	Address	Phone	Fax	Email	URL	Mission
Heart and Soul Animal Sanctuary	369 Montezuma Avenue, #130, Santa Fe, NM 87105-2626	505-455-2774	n/a	safeanimals2@ aol.com	http://www.ani-mal-sanctuary.org	mission is to alle-viate the suffer-ing of all animals
Homes for Hounds	5081 SW Pacific Coast Hwy, Waldport, OR	541-563-3467	n/a	silver@newport -net.com	http://www.homes forhounds.home-stead.com	an organization that finds homes for retired racing greyhounds
Horse Rescue	PO Box 232, Cushman, AR 72526	870-793-7534	870-793-5237	ozland@arkan-sas.net	http://myozland. tripod.com/ozland horserescue	a shelter for abused, ne-glected, or any other needy horses
Humane Society of the United States	2100 L Street NW, Washington, DC 20037	301-258-3072	301-258-3074	hwhite@hsus.org	http://www.hsus. org	the nation's larg-est animal protec-tion organization

Name	Address	Phone	Fax	Email	URL	Mission
International Society for Animal Rights	965 Griffin Pond Road, Clarks Summit, PA 18411	717-586-2200	717-586-9580	ISAR@AOL.COM	http://www.i-s-a-r.com	mission is to expose and end the injustice of the exploitation of animals and the suffering inflicted on them
International Wildlife Coalition	70 East Falmouth Highway, East Falmouth, MA 02536	508.548.8328	508.548.8542	iwcadopt@cape.com	http://www.iwc.org	mission is to save endangered species, protect wild animals and preserve wild habitat and the environment
Jane Goodall Institute	PO Box 14890, Silver Spring, MD 20911	301-565-0086	301-565-3188	cschluter@janegoodall.org	http://www.janegoodall.org	mission is to take informed and compassionate action to improve the environment of all living things

Name	Address	Phone	Fax	Email	URL	Mission
Jungle Friends	13915 N. State Road 121, Gainesville, FL 32653	904-462-7779	n/a	info@jungle friends.org	http://www.jungle friends.org	a refuge for primates against exploitation, abuse, neglect and improper care
K - 9 Rescue	652 Oak Trail, Lockhart, TX 78644	512-376-2499	603-307-0274	belmal@juno.com	http://www.k-9res cue.com	mission is saving dogs at the local shelter from death row
Last Chance For Animals	8033 Sunset Blvd., # 35, Los Angeles, CA 90046	310-271-6096	310-271-1890	office@lcanimal. org	http://www.lcanim al.org	mission is to promote certain basic rights protecting animals from pain caused by humans
League of Humane Voters	PO Box 401, Congers, NY 10920	845-268-8685	n/a	mail@humanevot ers.org	http://www.huma nevoters.org	established to organize voters who are concerned about non-human animals

Name	Address	Phone	Fax	Email	URL	Mission
Marine Mammal Center	The Marine Mammal Center, Golden Gate National Recreation Area, Salito, California 94965	n/a	415-289-SEAL	n/a	http://www.tmmc.org	one of the largest marine mammal rehabilitation facilities in the world
Medical Research Modernization Committee	3200 Morley Rd., Shaker Heights, OH 44122	216-283-6702	216-283-6702	stkaufman@pol.net	http://www.mrmcmed.org	a national health advocacy group composed of physicians, scientists and other health care professionals who evaluate the benefits, risks and costs of medical research methods and technologies
Montana Large Animal Sanctuary	PO Box 939, Polson, MT 59860	406-883-1823	406-883-1825	belkay@digisys.net	http://www.envirolink.org/orgs/mlasr	provides a loving home for large animals that are unwanted or require special care

Name	Address	Phone	Fax	Email	URL	Mission
National Anti-Vivisection Society	53 W. Jackson, Suite 1552, Chicago, IL 60604	800-888-NAVS	n/a	navs@navs.org	http://www.navs.org	mission is to abolish the exploitation of animals used in research, education and product testing
National Humane Education Society	521-A East Market Street, Leesburg, VA 20176	703/777-8319	703/771-4048	n/a	http://www.nhes.org	a nonprofit organization whose mission is to foster a sentiment of kindness to animals in children and adults
North Shore Animal League	25 Davis Avenue, Port Washington, NY 11050	516-883-7575	n/a	nsal1@aol.com	http://www.nsal.org	the largest pet adoption agency in the world
Northwest Animal Rights Network	1704 East Galer, Seattle, WA 98112	206-323-7301	n/a	info@narn.org	http://www.narn.org	mission is to actively promote the equal consideration of animals in the Pacific Northwest

Name	Address	Phone	Fax	Email	URL	Mission
People for Animal Rights	PO Box 8707, Kansas City, MO 64114	816-767-1199	n/a	parinfo@parkc.org	http://www.parkc.org	mission is to eliminate all animal abuse and exploitation
People for the Ethical Treatment of Animals (PETA)	501 Front Street, Norfolk, VA 23510	757-622-7382	757-622-0457	info@peta-online.org	http://www.peta.org	the largest animal rights organization in the world dedicated to establishing and protecting the rights of all animals.
Pets Alive	363 Derby Road, Middletown, NY 10940	845-386-9738	n/a	petsaliv@warwick.net	http://www.petsalive.com	a no-kill animal shelter whose mission is to rescue, rehabilitate, and place animals in need

Name	Address	Phone	Fax	Email	URL	Mission
Reptile & Exotic Animal Rescue	12184 Cr 167, Tyler, TX 75703	n/a	n/a	ReptileRescue1@cs.com	http://www.reptilerescue.tsx.org	a small non-profit organization dedicated to saving reptiles, exotic mammals and wildlife
Rocky Mountain Animal Defense	2525 Arapahoe, Suite E4-335, Boulder, CO 80302	303-449-4422	n/a	rmad@rmad.org	http://www.rmad.org	mission is to help eliminate the human-imposed suffering of animals in the Rocky Mountain region
Society for The Protection of Animals	PO Box 1047, Fremont, OH 43420	419-334-5521	n/a	spa@spaohio.org	http://www.spaohio.org	a non-profit organization created to provide a pro-active solution for minimizing the stray cat/dog population in the area

Name	Address	Phone	Fax	Email	URL	Mission
St. Louis Animal Rights Team	PO Box 28501, St. Louis, MO 63146	314-851-0928	n/a	stlouisanimalrigh tsteam@visto. com	http://www.enviro web.org/start	a nonprofit, educational, and activist organization dedicated to animal rights
Student Organization for Animal Rights	925 E. 900 S., Salt Lake City, UT 84105-1401	801-321-UARC	n/a	soar@uarc.com	http://soar.uarc. com	mission is to teach people that it is both easy and necessary to adopt a lifestyle that does not advocate the needless murder and torture of animals
The Animal Group	PO Box 250707, Little Rock, AR 72225	501-537-4824	801-327-5649	TheAnimalGroup @hotmail.org	http://www.theani malgroup.org	dedicated to promoting the humane treatment of animals and fostering respect, compassion and protection for all creatures

Name	Address	Phone	Fax	Email	URL	Mission
The Society for Animal Protective Legislation	PO Box 3719, Washington, DC 20007	202-337-2534	n/a	sapl@saplonline.org	http://www.saplonline.org	advocates legislation concerned with animal protection
Urban Wildlife Rescue	PO Box 201311, Denver, CO 80220	303-340-4911	303-363-8628	eartandme@visto.com	http://www.urbanwildliferescue.org	a non-profit organization dedicated to rescuing and rehabilitating wildlife
Voices For Animals	Stroudsburg, PA	570-992-6073	n/a	senne@ptd.net	http://voices.htmlplanet.com/main.html	small organization concerned with animal protection issues
Wildlife Advocacy Project	1601Connecticut Ave, NW #700, Washington, DC 20009	202-518-3700	202-588-5049	wildinfo@wildlifeadvocacy.org	http://www.wildlifeadvocacy.org	mission is to stop the abuse and exploitation of animals held in captivity
Wildlife Conservation Society	Bronx Zoo, 185th St. and Southern Blvd, Bronx, NY 10460	718-220-5197	n/a	feedback@wcs.org	http://www.wcs.org	mission is to save wildlife and wild lands throughout the world

Name	Address	Phone	Fax	Email	URL	Mission
World Animal Foundation	PO Box 30762, Middleburg Hts., OH 44130	530-685-6826	530-685-6826	CustomerService @WorldAnimal Foundation.com	http://www.World AnimalFoundation .com	mission is to preserve and protect the planet and the animal that inhabit it
World Wildlife Fund	1250 Twenty-Fourth Street N.W., PO Box 97180, Washington, DC 20037	1-800-CALL-WWF	n/a	n/a	http://www.world wildlife.org	the largest privately supported international conservation organization in the world whose mission is to protect the world's wildlife and wildlands
21st Century Animal Resource and Education Services	16224 N. Linda Dr., PO Box 373, Dolan Springs, AZ 86441	520-767-4895	same	21stcares@eresq. net	http://www.21stce nturycares.org	an animal welfare organization dedicated to supporting and promoting various forms of humane education in our nation's schools

GLOSSARY

Abandonment—The desertion of an animal due to lack of responsibility.

Adaptation—A change in the structure or function of an animal that produces better adjustment to the environment.

Animal Cruelty—Acts of violence or neglect perpetrated against animals, including overt abuse, dog fighting and cockfighting, and denying companion animals the basic necessities of care, such as food, water or shelter.

Animal Guardian—A term used by animal rights organizations to refer to an animal's owner.

Animal Hoarding or Collecting—Obsessive/compulsive disorder in which individual keeps a large number of animals and neglects to care for them.

Animal Neglect—The failure to provide an animal with the most basic requirements of food, water, shelter and veterinary care.

Animal Welfare Act—Act passed into law in 1966 that ensures that pets and animals used in research and for exhibition purposes are provided humane care and treatment.

At-risk Populations—People who may be at greater risk of getting sick from pets, including pregnant women, children under 5 years of age, organ transplant donees, cancer patients, and individuals with HIV/AIDS.

Backyard Breeder—Dog owner whose pet either gets bred by accident, or who breeds on purpose for a variety of reasons, e.g. to make money.

Boycott—To join together in refusing to deal with, so as to punish or coerce.

Canned Hunts—A barbaric practice in which hunters pay fees to shoot and kill exotic animals in a confined area from which they are unable to escape.

Captivity—The condition of being captive.

Cockfighting—A blood sport in which two roosters specifically bred for aggressiveness are placed beak to beak in a small ring and encouraged to fight to the death.

Crush Act—A federal law that prohibits people from knowingly creating, selling or possessing depictions of animal cruelty with the intent to place them in interstate or foreign commerce for commercial gain.

Dwarf Hamster—Refers to any species of hamster, such as the Chinese species, whose adult body size is substantially less than that attained by the Syrian or Golden species of hamsters.

Ear Cropping—The cropping of a purebred dog's ears to conform to a breed standard.

Endangered Species—Refers to those species defined in the Endangered Species Act (16 U.S.C. 1531 et seq.).

Environment—All the conditions, circumstances and influences surrounding an organism or group of organisms and affecting its development.

Euthanasia—The humane destruction of an animal accomplished by a method that produces rapid unconsciousness and subsequent death without evidence of pain or distress, or a method that utilizes anesthesia produced by an agent that causes painless loss of consciousness and subsequent death.

Exotic Animal—Any animal that is native to a foreign country or of foreign origin or character, is not native to the United States, or was introduced from abroad.

Experimentation—The process undertaken to discover something not yet known or to demonstrate or test something known.

Exploitation—To make use of or profit from something.

Extinction—The fact or state of being or becoming extinct; dying out, as of a species of animal.

Farm Animal—Any domestic species of cattle, sheep, swine, goats, llamas, or horses, which are normally and have historically, been kept and raised on farms in the United States, and used or intended for use as food or fiber, or for improving animal nutrition, breeding, management, or production efficiency, or for improving the quality of food or fiber. This term also includes animals such as rabbits, mink, and chinchilla, when they are used solely for purposes of meat or fur, and animals such as horses and llamas when used solely as work and pack animals.

Feral Cat—A cat too poorly socialized to be handled and who cannot be placed into a typical pet home.

Genus—A category that is used in classifying plants or animals that are similar in structure.

Habitat—The region where a plant or animal naturally grows or lives.

Humane—Kind, tender, merciful, sympathetic, etc.

Hybrid Cross—An animal resulting from the crossbreeding between two different species or types of animals. Crosses between wild animal species, such as lions and tigers, are considered to be wild animals. Crosses between wild animal species and domestic animals, such as dogs and wolves or buffalo and domestic cattle, are considered to be domestic animals.

Inherent—Existing in something as a natural or inseparable quality or right; inborn.

Intentional Animal Cruelty—Purposeful infliction of physical harm or injury on an animal.

Licensed Veterinarian—An individual who has graduated from an accredited school of veterinary medicine or has received equivalent formal education, and who has a valid license to practice veterinary medicine in some State.

Livestock—Domestic animals kept for use on a farm or raised for sale and profit.

Mammal—Any of a large class of warm-blooded vertebrates, generally with hair on the skin, whose offspring are fed with milk secreted by the female mammary glands.

Mandatory—Commanded or required by those in authority.

Monotype—The only type of its group.

Moratorium—Any authorized delay or stopping of some specified activity.

Painful Procedure—As it refers to animals, any procedure that would reasonably be expected to cause more than slight or momentary pain or distress in a human being to which that procedure was applied, that is, pain in excess of that caused by injections or other minor procedures.

Paralytic Drug—A drug which causes partial or complete loss of muscle contraction and which has no anesthetic or analgesic properties, so that the animal cannot move, but is completely aware of its surroundings and can feel pain.

Pet Animal—Any animal that has commonly been kept as a pet in family households in the United States, such as dogs, cats, guinea pigs, rabbits, and hamsters. This term excludes exotic animals and wild animals.

Poisoning—To harm or destroy by means of poison, a substance causing illness or death when eaten, drunk or absorbed in small quantities.

Pound—Also known as a shelter, refers to a facility that accepts and/or seizes animals for the purpose of caring for them, placing them through adoption, or carrying out law enforcement, whether or not the facility is operated for profit.

Puppy Mills—Breeding facilities that produce large numbers of purebred dogs that are regularly sold to pet shops across the country, and which have been criticized for overbreeding, inbreeding, poor veterinary care and overcrowding.

Random Source—Refers to dogs and cats obtained from animal pounds or shelters, auction sales, or from any person who did not breed and raise them on his or her premises.

Retail Pet Store—Any outlet where only the following animals are sold or offered for sale, at retail, for use as pets: Dogs, cats, rabbits, guinea pigs, hamsters, gerbils, rats, mice, gophers, chinchilla, domestic ferrets, domestic farm animals, birds, and cold-blooded species.

Soring—A type of show horse abuse whereby a mechanical or chemical agent is applied to the lower leg or hoof of a horse for the purpose of enhancing the animal's gait, i.e., forcing him to throw his front legs up and out.

Species—A group of highly similar plants or animals, part of a genus, that can reproduce fertile offspring only among themselves.

Statutory—Fixed by statute.

Sterilization—The act of making an animal incapable of producing others of its kind.

Stray—A currently or recently owned dog or cat who may be lost.

Subspecies—Any natural subdivision of a species that shows small differences in form from other subdivisions of the same species living in different regions.

Tail Docking—Cutting a purebred dog's tail to conform to a breed standard.

Taxonomy—The science of classifying things, such as plants and animals into natural, related groups, such as species and genera.

Total Animal Liberation—According to the organization, People for the Ethical treatment of Animals (PETA), total animal liberation refers to the idea that animals are not available to humans for food, clothing, entertainment, or medical advancement.

Trap/Neuter/Return (TNR)—A method of managing feral cat colonies that involves trapping the animals, spaying or neutering them, vaccinating them, and returning them to where they were found.

Vegan—The most extreme category of vegetarian whereby the individual does not eat beef, pork, poultry, mutton, eggs, dairy, honey, and gelatin, and also refuses to buy or use leather, wool, silk, fur, or any other animal-derived product.

Vegetarian—A person who chooses to eat no meat because of feelings against the killing of animals, or for reasons of health.

Vertebrate—Any of a large group of animals, including all mammals, fishes, birds, reptiles and amphibians, that have a backbone, brain and cranium.

Vivisection—Surgical operations or other experiments done on living animals for scientific purposes, as in studying diseases and trying to find cures for them.

Vivisectionist—A person who practices or favors the practice of vivisection for the good of science.

Weaned—Occurs when an animal has become accustomed to take solid food and has done so, without nursing, for a period of at least 5 days.

Wild animal—Any animal which is now or historically has been found in the wild, or in the wild state, within the boundaries of the United States, its territories, or possessions. This term includes, but is not limited to, animals such as: Deer, skunk, opossum, raccoon, mink, armadillo, coyote, squirrel, fox, wolf.

Wild State—Refers to an animal living in its original, natural condition; not domesticated.

Zoo—Any park, building, cage, enclosure, or other structure or premise in which a live animal or animals are kept for public exhibition or viewing, regardless of compensation.

Zoonotic—A disease that can be transmitted to humans.

BIBLIOGRAPHY AND ADDITIONAL RESOURCES

Animal and Plant Health Inspection Service (Date Visited: September 2006) <http://www.aphis.usda.gov/>.

American Society for the Prevention of Cruelty to Animals (Date Visited: September 2006) <http://www.aspca.org/>.

The Humane Society of the United States (Date Visited: September 2006) <http://www.hsus.org/>.

Black's Law Dictionary, Fifth Edition. St. Paul, MN: West Publishing Company, 1979.

Centers for Disease Control (Date Visited: September 2006) <http://www.cdc.gov/>.

National Association for Biomedical Research (Date Visited: September 2006) <http://www.nabr.org/>.

National Centers for Infectious Disease (Date Visited: September 2006)<http://www.cdc.gov/ncidod/>.

National Institute of Health (Date Visited: September 2006) <http://www.nih.gov/>.

United States Department of Agriculture (Date Visited: September 2006) <http://www.usda.gov/>.

United States Fish and Wildlife Service (Date Visited: September 2006) <http://www.fws.gov/>.